T0194060

UNVEILING THE MYSTERY OF THE BRIDE OF CHRIST

THE RESTORATION TRUTH OF WHO & WHAT IS THE BRIDE OF CHRIST

DUKE LEVY JR.

WESTBOW
PRESS®
A DIVISION OF THOMAS NELSON
& ZONDERVAN

Scripture quotations marked (NIV) are taken from the Holy Bible, New International Version®, NIV®. Copyright © 1973, 1978, 1984, 2011 by Biblica, Inc.™ Used by permission of Zondervan. All rights reserved worldwide. www. zondervan.com The "NIV" and "New International Version" are trademarks registered in the United States Patent and Trademark Office by Biblica, Inc.™

All scriptures are taken from the King James Version of the Bible unless noted otherwise.

WestBow Press books may be ordered through booksellers or by contacting:

WestBow Press
A Division of Thomas Nelson & Zondervan
1663 Liberty Drive
Bloomington, IN 47403
www.westbowpress.com
1 (866) 928-1240

Cover design by Chae Saucier.

ISBN: 978-1-9736-1892-8 (sc)
ISBN: 978-1-9736-1894-2 (hc)
ISBN: 978-1-9736-1893-5 (e)

Library of Congress Control Number: 2018902269

Print information available on the last page.

WestBow Press rev. date: 03/20/2018

CONTENTS

AUTHOR'S STATEMENT

In 2010, I began putting thoughts on paper as a means of ministering to myself. Writing a book was the farthest thing from my mind. Two years prior (2008), God was stirring up my spirit to take a fresh look at His Word again, allowing me to go deeper in my understanding of His truths.

As I began writing what I was learning, my understanding and focus was directed to a special people who are close to the heart of the Father, a people known as the Bride of Christ.

What you will be reading in this book is a result of a work which began in 2010, basically completed in 2012, with the final touches made in 2017. Having worked on the book for the past seven years, I believe now is the right time to seek publication.

So as we enter a time for our nation to be under the presidency of Donald Trump, a man termed by Dr. Lance Wallnau as a "wrecking ball to the spirit of political correctness", my hope and prayer is that this book will prove to be a "wrecking ball" to the spirit of religious correctness, challenging the believer to rethink some previously held beliefs which do not agree with the holy scriptures.

DEDICATION

I dedicate this book to our great heavenly Father, who authored it. I just put it down on paper. I say that with conviction because thoughts did not begin to flow until I put pen to paper.

In other words, the truth contained within these pages did not come out of my mind but from the mind of Christ within me, led and inspired by God's Holy Spirit.

I am humbled and honored to be used for this purpose.

PREFACE

There is a fascinating prophecy in the Bible that should excite all Christian believers, particularly as we realize we are living in the last days. It is found in Acts 3:19-21. The thrust of the prophecy is this:

That Jesus Christ must remain in heaven until the restitution (restoring) "of all things which God has spoken by the mouth of all his holy prophets since the world began."

The word *restitution* or *restoring* means to bring back into existence or to reestablish.

What is exciting is that we are seeing today this prophecy being fulfilled right before our eyes. God is restoring or reestablishing the truth of His Word back to His people. The veil is being lifted; the scales of blindness are coming off for "those who have eyes to see."

Through this book, God is restoring (bringing back into existence) an amazing and extraordinary truth that has been hidden for millennia and is now being reestablished, in these last days. The early church knew and understood that God, through His Holy Spirit, was preparing a people, a special group, who would embrace this truth and qualify to rule and reign with Christ at His return when the kingdom (government) of God would be set up on the earth. This special group is called the Bride of Christ.

The early church was kingdom minded. Their hearts were not set on going to heaven. The preparation message was not only at the centerpiece of Christ's kingdom message ("repent, for the Kingdom of God is at hand"-see Mark:14-15) but was at the centerpiece of all the letters written by the apostles.

For example, in the apostles' letters, such as in the book of Romans, 1 and 2 Peter, James, and 1, 2, and 3 John, we see a heavy emphasis on sanctified or righteous living, a message that is crucial in the preparation of the Bride.

The restorational truth of the mystery of the Bride (who and what is the Bride of Christ) must be told in these last days in preparation of the Bride and in advanced of the return of Christ. Jesus is preparing for His Bride now.

Notice what He says in John 14:2-3:

> In my Father's house are many mansions: If it were not so, I would have told you. I go to prepare a place for you.
>
> And if I go and prepare a place for you, I will come again, and receive you unto myself; that where I am, there you may be also.

Do you know where Jesus Christ is going to be and who these people are that He desires to be with wherever He goes? This book answers those questions. The truth about the Bride is truth restored (truth re-established), which must be told so that the Father can release Jesus from heaven soon, to set up His glorious kingdom.

It is in this light that this book is presented.

FOREWORD

For many in organized Christianity today, the subject of the Bride of Christ and how the Bride fits into the plan of God is a mystery because the true message of the Bride has been kept hidden and is not being taught today. If it is taught, it is generally mentioned in the context of the rapture (the taking away) of the church, where God is going to rapture His church, the Bride, to heaven to escape the wrath to come over all the earth.

However, for me, understanding who the Bride is has been different. Over the years, God, by His grace, has given me a unique perspective in which to view His plan for mankind, which centers on a special relationship with a special people called the Bride of Christ. This understanding of the Bride is key to understanding the whole plan of God for mankind, particularly as it involves the kingdom of God.

Jesus first brought me into a relationship with Him by calling me into a conservative Christian fellowship, whose main focus was the kingdom of God and living by the laws of the kingdom.

I grew in love with my heavenly Father and my Savior, Jesus Christ, getting to know them intimately through walking the sanctified life. Later on in life, the Father introduced me to His Holy Spirit, and a whole new world of intimacy opened up to me. I spent time with the Father through his Holy Spirit's tangible presence, walked in the Father's anointing, receiving and operating in His gifts, and was blessed by His grace. From this background and perspective (illuminated by the Holy Spirit), God has allowed me to see many things in the organized Christian church today that are not in agreement with His Word.

You see, I look into the Word of God, the Bible, not with traditional Protestant thinking glasses, where the focus is on going to heaven, but with "kingdom glasses", where the focus is getting ready for God's kingdom (His government) to come to earth. Do you remember the Lord's Prayer, where Jesus taught His disciples to pray: "Thy Kingdom come, Thy will be done, on earth as it is in heaven" (Matt. 6:10)? We are to pray for God's kingdom to come to earth.

I see a Creator God with kingdom on His mind, starting from the book of Genesis all the way through the book of Revelation. Did you know that Jesus was given a special message from the Father to be proclaimed on the earth? That is why Jesus is called the Messenger of the Covenant. Notice Malachi 3:1:

> Behold, I [God] will send my messenger [announcing the coming of the messiah], and he shall prepare the way before me: and the Lord [Messiah] whom you seek, shall suddenly come to his temple, even the messenger of the covenant, whom you delight in: behold, he [Jesus the Messiah] shall come [with the message of the covenant] saith the Lord of hosts.

The message Jesus came with was a kingdom message. Jesus said, "I must preach the Kingdom of God to other cities … For therefore am I sent" (Luke 4:43). His message centered around the kingdom of God coming to earth, which involved repentance and returning back to covenant living. Notice Mark 1:15:

> The time is fulfilled, and the Kingdom of God is at hand: repent ye [change your mind-set—turn back to covenant living] and believe the gospel [the good news that the Kingdom of God has arrived].

Do you know why Jesus was born? No, it wasn't to come and save us. Let's allow Jesus to tell us the reason He was born. Notice His answer to Pontius Pilate when Pilate asked him, "Are you a king?"

Jesus answered: "You say that I am a king. To this end was I born and for this cause came I into the world, that I should bear witness unto the truth. Every one that is of the truth hears my voice" (John 18:37).

Are you hearing His voice today about kingship and the kingdom of God? While on earth, Jesus lived out a life which qualified Him to be king. He set the way, the example for us to follow.

Jesus said in John 12:26, "If any man serve me, let him follow me," which means "live like I live." The apostle Paul understood this. He wrote, "Be you followers of me as I follow Christ" (1 Cor. 11:1).

Every Christmas season, Christian churchgoers hear and recite the popular scripture in Isaiah 9:6, which says:

For unto us a child is born, unto us a son is given: and the government shall be upon his shoulder: and his name shall be called Wonderful, Counsellor, The mighty God, The everlasting Father, The Prince of Peace.

Yet how many people do not truly understand what that verse means? Do you see the connection of Christ's birth and the coming of the kingdom (government) of God on earth? The church today is not hearing a kingdom message. The church teaches about the messenger but not about His message, which has everything to say about the kingdom of God and our part in it.

This book is about the kingdom of God. It is about Father God preparing a Bride to rule and reign with His Son, Jesus Christ, when He comes to set up His kingdom on earth. Yet this book is more.

It is about restored truth. It is about a way of life. It is about a mystery that has lain dormant from the first century of the church and is now being revealed. It is about a mystery that, when fully understood and embraced, will captivate and motivate believers into achieving their destinies as ordained by Creator God.

When the message of who and what is the Bride of Christ is understood, it will reveal the true purpose of life; it will not only reveal why mankind was placed on this earth, but more importantly, it will explain why you have been born for such a time as this.

INTRODUCTION

There are several opinions about who or what is the Bride of Christ. Some believe that the bride is the city, New Jerusalem, as mentioned in Revelation 21:9-10. Many believe (and it is widely taught as doctrine) that all the church is the Bride. Many are taught and have faith that if you are a believer in Jesus Christ, then you are part of the Bride and will be raptured away to heaven, which will be your eternal home.

Just what is the truth about the Bride of Christ? Does the Bible reveal in no uncertain terms who or what is the Bride and the role it will play for all eternity? The simple answer is, Yes, it does. And that is what this book is all about.

The chapters in this book are designed to challenge you, the reader, in your thinking and in your belief system. Many of you may not want to finish this book because the points made will go contrary to what you have been taught and believed. I urge you to not give up. For far too long, the organized church has accepted as true doctrine some teachings which, when held up to the light of truth of the inspired written Word of God, do not agree with the scriptures; this is particularly true concerning the Bride of Christ.

The Bride has a special role in the kingdom of God: ruling and reigning with Christ for one thousand years and beyond. As you read this book, it is important to keep this one point paramount in your mind:

Becoming a part of the Bride of Christ is about reward. It is "the prize of the high calling of God in Christ Jesus" (Phil. 3:14). Unlike salvation, which is based upon faith, becoming a part of the Bride is based upon how you live while on this earth.

It is the primary thesis of this book (and will be shown conclusively to be true) that not all who claim to be believers will be the Bride and that there are conditions which must be met by the believer to qualify to be the Bride of Christ. Remember that qualifying to be the Bride is about reward, not salvation. Salvation is the gift of God (Rom. 6:23); it cannot be earned.

There is a profound scripture which bears out this truth about qualifying to be the Bride, and it is found in Revelation 19:7-8:

> Let us be glad and rejoice, and give honor to him: for the marriage of the Lamb is come and his wife hath made herself ready.

Here we see the Bridegroom, Jesus Christ, marrying His Bride, and it says that the Bride (His wife) "has made herself ready." That statement tells us that this special group (His wife) took personal responsibility in preparing herself for the marriage.

What was special about the Bride? What did she have to do to prepare herself to be worthy enough to be the Bride? The answer is revealed in verse 8:

> And to her was granted that she should be arrayed in fine linen, clean and white: for the fine linen is the righteousness of saints.

The Bride was declared righteous. How? Could it have been by how she lived her life on earth (her preparation)?

To cover this subject, I will be dealing with a few sacred cows, mainstream Christian doctrines and interpretations that have been accepted as truth yet do not line up with the clear Word of God. It is not my intention, nor is it my purpose, to malign or demean any denomination or ministry that holds dearly to these teachings. It is time for the Body of Christ to re-examine certain doctrines and interpretations, which have been traditionally held but do not line up with the Word of God. We are living in the "times of restitution [restoring] of all things" (Acts 3:21); God is restoring truth back into his church.

It is my goal and purpose to clear up the mystery of the Bride by leading you on a journey through the scriptures to show you without a shadow of doubt who the Bride is and what her preparation is all about.

The teaching that will be presented is not new truth—it is restored truth, truth that laid hidden but is now being reestablished. Through a "precept upon precept, precept upon precept, line upon line, line upon line, here a little, there a little" (Isa. 28:10) approach, nuggets of truth will be revealed, layers of understanding will be pealed backed over scriptures you have heard about, studied, or perhaps never understood, giving you clarity of God's Word as never before. Even if you are a novice to God's Word, it is my desire to make the truth understandable.

My approach to teaching and understanding the Word of God is to let the Bible interpret itself, that is, to let the Bible interpret its own words or symbols, rather than inject a personal opinion or bias. At times, I will be using the New Strong's Expanded Exhaustive Concordance of the Bible (2001), to expand and enrich the meaning of certain Hebrew or Greek words.

Are you ready to go on a treasure hunt, seeking nuggets of truth that will change your life forever?

This is what has happened to me over the past forty years of studying the Holy Bible: God has taken me on a treasure hunt through His Word, helping me to discover things that were hidden (see chapter 11 on the hidden things of God), removing the blinders, and giving me eyes to see and ears to hear what the Holy Spirit is revealing and saying to the true believers today. A huge nugget God has allowed me to see in His Word is who and what is the Bride of Christ. I was stunned and amazed as God's Holy Spirit guided me in connecting the dots. By His grace, God helped me to see His Word in a whole new light; and I want to share with you these nuggets.

Now, I want you to realize that I take very seriously what God says about His Word. He makes it very clear that we are not to add to or take away from His inspired Word (Deut. 4:2). If I cannot make a clear connection with God's Word in bringing out these nuggets (letting the Word interpret the Word), I will emphatically indicate that this is what I believe, my opinion.

It will take courage to believe the truth. The Bible tells us that Satan, the devil, "deceiveth the whole world" (Rev. 12:9), and that includes the Christian world—the church. But praise God. The light of truth is shining on the deception of the devil and the truth of the Bride is being revealed.

It is my sincere prayer for you, the reader, that the great God of the universe will grant you eyes to see and ears to hear what His Holy Spirit is revealing and saying to His church (his called-out ones) today; that you may fulfill your destiny to be a part of the Bride of Christ.

FALSE HOPE, FALSE EXPECTATIONS

Many believers in organized Christian churches today have bought into a false concept of who and what is the Bride of Christ, giving them false hope and false expectations that could cost them dearly, even their own salvation. Let me explain.

God's Word tells us in 2 Thessalonians 2:3 that in the end time, there will be a "great falling away" from the faith:

> Let no man deceive you by any means: for that day [the day of Christ's return to earth] shall not come, except there come a falling away first.

That means many will turn their backs on Jesus and the truth of His Word. Jesus Himself asked the question: "When he comes, will he find faith on the earth?" (Luke 18:8).

Please understand this fact: Deception is alive and well in the Christian ranks. Jesus Christ gives a powerful warning to His people in Matthew 24:4–5, a warning that pertains to deception in the end times we are now living:

> Take heed that no man deceive you. For *many* shall come
> in my name, saying, I am Christ, and shall *deceive many.*
> (emphasis added)

In this verse, Jesus is not talking about individuals who would proclaim that they themselves are Jesus Christ. Those who do claim to be Christ are "not many" and are laughed to scorn, never taken seriously by the populace.

Jesus states very clearly and emphatically in these verses to "take heed," or to put it another way, "pay close attention to what I am telling you so that no person will deceive you." Jesus goes on to say that "many [not a few] shall come in my name," which means that many will come proclaiming to represent Him—such as pastors, teachers, apostles, prophets, or evangelists—saying this is who Jesus is, and "shall deceive many." These deceivers will teach a false message during the end time that will include a false message about the Bride, leading many believers to have false hope and false expectations.

Now, please understand: It is not my intent to bash other ministers or ministries. However, there is a popular teaching about the Bride of Christ that is gaining momentum in these last days among mainstream evangelical Protestant and charismatic Pentecostal churches, a teaching that does not agree with the true Word of God. The message goes something like this:

If you are a believer in Jesus, then you are a member of the Bride of Christ, and you will not have to go through the Great Tribulation, a horrific time prophesized in the Bible, when all hell breaks loose on the earth just prior to the return of Christ. You will be raptured, or taken to heaven, to escape the great torment that is going to happen to all those left behind on earth.

The truth of the matter is this: Jesus will indeed protect those chosen to be His Bride, but it will not be *every* believer. This fact will be shown in the chapters ahead. There will only be a few ("Many are called, but *few* are chosen," Matt. 20:16; emphasis added) who will be protected when compared to the millions who profess faith in Jesus Christ. Many believers will have to go through hell on earth, paying the ultimate price of losing their lives (but not their salvation). When that time arrives, many will be shocked when they realize what they have been taught and believed about escaping the wrath to come was not true, giving them false hope and false expectations. And unfortunately, because of the deception, many believers will be tempted to turn away from their faith in Jesus, as we read above in 2 Thessalonians 2:3.

I want to give you a biblical example of believers who were led astray in their belief systems (given false hope and expectations) and did not receive the promise of reward they thought they were entitled. They were completely shocked.

The account is in Luke 13:24–28. A more thorough explanation of these verses is given in chapter 6 ("Torah"). For now, here is a brief synopsis of what Jesus was teaching:

On the Day of Judgment, when rewards are given, there will be many believers who will be on the outside looking in. They will desire to be with Christ wherever He is but will not be able to. They will be shut out of the kingdom, to their utter amazement and disbelief.

They will justify themselves by saying, "Lord, we have experienced Your presence by the Holy Spirit and have been taught about You in the churches; we received salvation and were told that salvation was all that was needed for us to be the bride and to enter into Your kingdom where you will be."

Then Jesus shall tell them, "I don't know where you are from; I don't know you. I didn't have an intimate relationship with you." Jesus tells them that "even though you are believers in Me [you are saved], you are strangers to Me because you are workers of unrighteousness [meaning, you did not walk in obedience to My Word, My commandments]. So consequently, you are thrust out of My kingdom on earth." (More is given on the importance of obedience in chapters 5 and 6.)

Notice the reaction of the believers when they realized they were misled and believed a lie:

> *There shall be weeping and gnashing of teeth,* when you shall
> see Abraham, and Isaac, and Jacob, and all the prophets in
> the Kingdom of God, and *you yourselves thrust out.* (Luke
> 13:28, emphasis added)

Look at what Jesus says in Matthew 7:21:

> Not *every one* [not every believer] that says unto me, Lord,
> Lord, shall enter into the kingdom of heaven; but *he that
> does the will on my Father which is in heaven.*

You must understand that the context here is that Jesus is speaking of *reward*, not salvation. Entering the kingdom of heaven means coming into the kingdom (government) of God on earth as His Bride, where He will be ruling with His Bride for a thousand years and beyond.

In the chapters ahead, you are going to learn what the will of the Father is for your life. He has great things in store for you. To be able to enter into the kingdom of God requires you to be the Bride, the greatest reward given by your heavenly Father. God's Word tells us that "eye has not seen, nor ear heard, neither have entered into the heart of man, the things which God (the Father) has prepared for them that love Him" (1 Cor. 2:9).

Do you love your heavenly Father? Do you love your Savior and soon coming King, Jesus Christ? This book is about how important it is to show your love for God by walking in obedience to His Word. Your Father is in the heart business, not lip service. Your life on this earth is important to Him. As your Father, He has given you life "to prove you, to know what is in your heart, whether you will keep His commandments or not" (Deut. 8:2).

Believe this: It is God's desire for you to be a part of the Bride of Christ. That is why you are reading this book. He does not want you to have any false hope or false expectations.

LOOKING THROUGH KINGDOM GLASSES

What many people do not realize is that the Bible is a kingdom book, and understanding who and what is the Bride is centered around the concept of kingdom.

It is unfortunate that we in the Western world are ignorant in understanding the concept of kingdom. For most, the only idea of a kingdom would be derived from going to the Magic Kingdom or the Animal Kingdom at Disney World. Yet the understanding of what a kingdom is, is pivotal to understanding what the Bible is all about.

Basically, a kingdom is a government that has rule over a people on the earth. A kingdom has a ruler, the king, who rules over a domain (land), has a constituency (citizens), and has a law (constitution).

We see at the very beginning of the Bible how the Creator God, after creating the earth, created man in His image, after His likeness, for the purpose of establishing the kingdom (government) of God on earth. We read this in Genesis 1:26:

> And God said, Let us make man in our image, after our likeness: and let them have *dominion* [rulership and authority] over the fish of the sea, and over the fowl of the

air, and over the cattle, and *over all the earth.* (emphasis added)

The Bible tells about Satan, the devil, and his evil kingdom and how he attempted to thwart the plan of God by getting the first Adam to commit treason against the kingdom of God, by turning over his God-given authority to Satan, who became the "god [or ruler] of this world" (2 Cor. 4:4).

But God had a plan. He was not taken off guard by Adam's disobedience, which resulted in the loss of God's kingdom on earth. From that point on, God put into motion His redemptive work, in which He would reestablish His kingdom on earth through the last Adam, Jesus Christ, enabling man's authority on earth to be reinstated.

The centerpiece of the Bible story is how God worked through one man, Abraham, to raise up a nation, Israel, to bring forth the birth of His Son, Jesus (the last Adam), to qualify to be king and to restore the kingdom of God back to earth.

Few realize that Jesus was *sent* to earth with a message from God the Father. What was His message? It was the "message of the covenant" (see Mal. 3:1). What was the message of the covenant about? It was the good news (the gospel) about the kingdom of God and living by the laws of the kingdom. Notice what Jesus says in Luke 4:43:

> I must preach the *Kingdom of God* to other cities … For therefore [for this reason] *am I sent.* (emphasis added)

Everywhere Jesus went, He taught in parables about the kingdom of God. He sent out his twelve disciples to preach one message: the kingdom of God.

> Then he [Jesus] called his twelve disciples together, and gave them power and authority over all devils and to cure diseases. And he sent them to preach the kingdom of God, and to heal the sick. And they departed, and went through

the towns, preaching the gospel [of the kingdom of God] and healing every where. (Luke 9:1, 2, 6)

Are you beginning to see a pattern here of where Jesus's focus was? Just before He ascended to heaven, Jesus taught His apostles for forty days on the "things pertaining to the Kingdom of God" (Acts 1:3).

It is important to make the connection between covenant and kingdom because this was Jesus's message. For example, when Jesus emphasized keeping the commandments of God (see Matt. 19:17 and John 14:15), He was teaching about walking in covenant relationship with God the Father, which meant living in harmony with the laws of the kingdom of God. That is what righteousness is all about, being in "right standing" with the laws of God. (Remember that Jesus is teaching about how to live on earth and not about salvation, which is by faith.)

But this is so awesome: Jesus's message of the kingdom includes the destiny of the believer. You see, Jesus wants to share rulership of His kingdom with a very special people, called His Bride. Please notice what Jesus says in His message to the churches (Rev. 3:21):

> To him [or her] that overcomes [this will be the Bride], will I grant to sit with me in my throne [in the Kingdom of God on earth], even as I also overcame, and am set down with my Father in His throne [in heaven].

Here are a few powerful prophetic scriptures that highlight the kingdom theme of the Bible, revealing the soon coming kingdom (government) of God to this earth, being ruled over by Jesus Christ, King of kings, and Lord of lords, sharing rulership with those who qualified (His Bride), His special called-out and chosen ones:

> And in the days of these kings [in the last days] shall the God of heaven set up a kingdom, which shall never be destroyed; and the kingdom shall not be left to other people [rulership will be given to the Bride], but it shall

break in pieces and consume all these kingdoms, and it shall stand for ever (Dan. 2:44).

And there was given him [Jesus] dominion, and glory, and a kingdom, that all people, nations, and languages, should serve him: his dominion is an everlasting dominion, which shall not pass away, and his kingdom that which shall not be destroyed (Dan. 7:14).

But the saints [the Bride] of the most High shall take the kingdom, and possess the kingdom for ever, even for ever and ever (Dan. 7:18).

Until the Ancient of days came, and judgment was given to the saints [the Bride] of the most High: and the time came that the saints [the Bride] possessed the kingdom (Dan. 7:22).

And the kingdom and dominion, and the greatness of the kingdom under the whole heaven, shall be given to the people of the saints [the Bride] of the most High, whose kingdom is an everlasting kingdom, and all dominions shall serve and obey him (Dan. 7:27).

Note: The Hebrew word translated *saints* in Daniel has the meaning of "one devoted or dedicated to a particular purpose or one being set apart for the work of God" (see Strong's #6918 and #6942).

And he [or she] that overcometh, and keepeth my works [obeys the commandments of God] unto the end, to him [the Bride] will I give power [authority] over the nations (Rev. 2:26).

And hast made us [the Bride] unto our God kings and priests: and we shall reign on the earth (Rev. 5:10).

These shall make war with the Lamb [in the end time],
and the Lamb shall overcome them; for he is Lord of lords,
and King of kings; and they that are with him [the Bride]
are called, and chosen, and faithful (Rev. 17:14).

Yet there is another concept of kingdom embedded in the truth of who and what is the Bride of Christ. This truth has to do with understanding the God kingdom, the divine Family, consisting of God the Father, Jesus the Son, and the children of God.

The Bride is called the firstfruits, or the first to be born again into the God Family (see chapter 8 for more information on the firstfruits).

Is this helping you to see that the Bible is a kingdom book? The only way you can truly understand the Word of God and His plan for mankind, which includes the purpose of the Bride, is by looking through kingdom glasses. Now, do you have yours on?

THE JEWELS OF GOD

In the book of Malachi, there is a nugget of truth that has escaped the attention of the Christian church today.

Starting with verse 16 of chapter 3, we see a very special group, a special people reserved unto God. Beginning in verse 16 and continuing on to the end of chapter 4, we are going to read about a group of believers who are very near and dear to the heart of God, a group He calls "His jewels."

But first, we need to realize that it is no accident that the book of Malachi is positioned at the end of what is called the Old Testament. Here we see the divine hand of God at work as He uses this book of prophecy as a bridge to link the Old Testament with the New Testament. Many Christians discount the Old Testament scriptures as irrelevant for the church today. Sadly, many in the church devote little time to studying or reading in the Old Testament, seeing no significance other than the scriptures are nice stories to talk about in Sunday school.

What many fail to see in the Old Testament is how God chose a people, the nation Israel, the descendants of Abraham, Isaac, and Jacob, to be above all nations, to be a holy (separate) nation, not because of their greatness or that they were better than anyone else, but because of the devotion and obedience of one man, Abraham. Notice this awesome calling in Exodus 19:5-6:

> Now therefore, if ye will obey my voice indeed, and keep my covenant [walk in covenant relationship], then ye shall be a peculiar treasure unto me above all people: for all the earth is mine:
>
> And ye shall be unto me a kingdom of priests [you shall be my royal rulers, having dominion], and an holy nation [dedicated and set apart people for my purposes].

But the calling of Abraham's descendants to greatness was conditional. Did you notice the word *if*: "If you will obey," "If you keep."

From these scriptures, we can see God's desire to have a special people, a peculiar treasure, a royal family unto Himself. Yet God knew that not all Israel would meet the challenge and walk in covenant relationship with Him.

Deuteronomy 5:29 says:

> O that there were such an heart in them, that they would fear me, and keep all my commandments always, that it might be well with them, and with their children for ever!

The nation Israel, as a whole, missed their destiny of being a peculiar treasure. Malachi 3:7 points this out:

> Even from the days of your fathers ye [the nation Israel] are gone away from mine ordinances, and have not kept them.

Yet God was going to have a "peculiar treasure" unto Himself. The scene changes at Malachi 3:16. Here we see a special group. Now you will need to take off your traditional Protestant thinking glasses and begin to look at these scriptures through kingdom thinking glasses.

Then they that feared the LORD spake often one to another: and the LORD hearkened, and heard it, and a book of remembrance was written before him for them that feared the LORD, and that thought [meditated] upon his name [His character].

Here, at the close of the Old Testament, God centers in on a special people, those who "feared the Lord," whose names were written in a book of remembrance (not the Book of Life), and who "thought upon his name." Please understand this nugget of truth. The expression "they that feared the Lord" means "they that kept the commandments of God" (see Deut. 5:29 above).

God's focus continues on this special group in verse 17 of Malachi 3:

And they shall be mine, saith the LORD of hosts, in that day when I make up my jewels; and I will spare them, as a man spareth his own son that serveth him.

Did you see in these verses a very special called-out people who feared the Lord, had their names written in a book of remembrance, a people God says shall be His jewels and He will protect them?

Did you notice in Exodus 19:5 above where God sets the conditions to be chosen as His "peculiar treasure"? The Hebrew word translated *peculiar treasure* is Strong's word #5459. It means "possession, signifying property in the sense of a private possession, one personally acquired and carefully preserves." It is the same Hebrew word translated *jewels* in Malachi 3:17. So let's go back to Exodus 19:5 and insert the word *jewels*:

Now therefore, if you will obey my voice indeed, and keep my covenant, then you shall be jewels unto me, above all people: for all the earth is mine.

God's conditions to be chosen His jewels are simple: Obey His voice and keep His covenant (Exod. 19:5). We will develop this point about how we qualify to be God's jewels as we go through the chapters ahead. The main point we need to see at this juncture is that the Bride is hidden here in Malachi under the guise of those who feared God, whose names are written in the book of remembrance, and who are known as God's "peculiar treasure" (His jewels).

It has been God's desire from the beginning to have a special people close to Him, a people "above all people," a royal family, who walk in intimate relationship with Him, who obey His voice and keep His covenant, who love Him and express that love, loyalty, and allegiance to Him by walking in complete obedience and harmony with His Word. (I will express in greater detail this love, loyalty, and allegiance for God in chapter 7 because it is paramount in our understanding the mystery of the Bride.)

Let's continue in the book of Malachi, chapter 4, where we will see that God is going to give specific instructions to His jewels (His Bride), and then God will prophesy that He will sovereignly move in the end time to ensure that He will have a Bride (a peculiar treasure, His Jewels), lest He come and "smite the earth with a curse."

In chapter 4, verse 1, we see that the setting for what follows in the remaining verses is the last days, when the wicked shall be destroyed. Verses 2 and 3 refer again to those who fear God's name (His jewels), who will "tread down the wicked; for they shall be ashes under the soles of [their] feet in the day that [God] shall do this."

Now look at verse 4. Here God gives a very special instruction to His jewels:

> Remember ye the law [Torah] of Moses my servant, which
> I commanded unto him in Horeb for all Israel, with the
> statutes and judgments.

Notice what God says here to His Bride (do you have your kingdom glasses on?): "Remember the law of Moses." Now don't choke on these words. This is vital because it involves walking in covenant relationship. It involves keeping the laws of the kingdom. Living by the laws of God bring blessings. The father of the faithful, Abraham, loved and honored God.

How? He obeyed God's laws, commandments, and statutes. Notice what God says about him (Gen. 26:5):

> Abraham obeyed my voice, and kept my charge, my commandments, my statutes, and my laws.

A Major Shift Is Required

Notice how God ends this prophecy in Malachi, which pertains to the times we are living in now.

> Behold, I will send you Elijah the prophet before the coming of the great and dreadful day of the LORD:
>
> And he shall turn the heart of the fathers to the children, and the heart of the children to their fathers, lest I come and smite the earth with a curse.

Why must Elijah come in the last days? Why is this important? Jesus answers this question in Matthew 17:11:

> And Jesus answered and said unto them, [Elijah] truly shall first come, and restore all things.

What was Jesus talking about when He said, "Elijah shall first come and restore all things"? The term *restore all things* refers to restoring the children of Israel (the believers) back to covenant relationship with their God. Notice the meaning of the word *restore* used in the above verse:

"This word is used of the divine restoration of Israel and conditions affected by it, including the renewal of the covenant broken by them; [it is used] of giving or bringing a person back" (from Strong's word #600).

To prepare the way for Christ's first coming, John the Baptist came "in the spirit and power of Elijah" (Luke 1:15–17) to restore the children of Israel back to covenant relationship with their God, which meant turning their hearts (the people's mind-set) back to the written Torah. John's message was "Repent: change your mind-set and turn your heart back to God" (see Matt. 3:1-8).

This same "restore all things" must take place again prior to Christ's second coming, only this time, it will be done by a company of prophets (those individuals and ministries God will be using in the latter days), operating in the spirit of Elijah, turning the hearts of the "fathers to the children and the children to the fathers."

Now, let's return to the prophecy in Malachi, chapter 4, and understand its true meaning.

In Malachi 4:6, God says "he shall turn the heart of the fathers to the children and the heart of the children to their fathers." Please understand: This prophecy is not about restoring family relationships. This is a profound prophecy of what God is going to do just prior to the return of Jesus Christ back to this earth.

Now, let's understand who the fathers are. We must allow the Bible to define its own terms. In 1 Corinthians 10:1, we find the answer: "Moreover, brethren, I would not that ye should be ignorant, how that all our fathers were under the cloud, and all passed through the sea." Did you catch that? The fathers are the descendants of Abraham, the nation Israel. Paul was reminding his people about the time the nation Israel left Egypt, were guided by the cloud by day, and miraculously passed through the Red Sea to escape from Pharaoh's army (Exod. 13, 14).

Who are the children? Galatians 3:7 says, "Know ye therefore that they which are of faith [in Jesus], the same are the children of Abraham." The children of Abraham are the believers in Christ.

God is saying in no uncertain terms that unless Israel (those Jews who are under the Old Covenant and keep the laws of God) turn their hearts toward the believers in Christ (those who have accepted Jesus as their Savior) and the believers in Christ turn their heart toward the Jews, who keep God's commandments, He will come and "smite the earth with a curse." Why is this so important? It all has to do with God the Father desiring a Bride for His Son, Jesus, a Bride comprised of Jews and Gentiles, who will be faithful, loyal, and obedient, just as Christ was faithful, loyal, and obedient to His Father.

To back up and support this interpretation of the prophecy in Malachi 4, I want to direct your attention to two significant events recorded in the New Testament, events that seem to be totally unrelated, yet are divinely connected:

- the appearance of the angel Gabriel before Zacharias, the father of John the Baptist (Luke 1:11-17)
- the transfiguration of Jesus with Moses and Elijah (Mark 9:1-10)

In the appearance of the angel Gabriel, where Gabriel announces to Zacharias that he will have a son who "shall be great in the sight of the Lord," we learn about the work of a prophet operating in the "spirit and power of Elijah." Notice what happens under this anointing:

> Many of the children of Israel shall he turned to the Lord
> their God (verse 16).

This is a reference to John the Baptist turning the believers back to covenant relationship, back to the commandments of God. How will he do it?

> And he [John the Baptist] shall go before him [God] in the
> spirit and power of [Elijah] to turn the hearts of the fathers
> [covenant Israel] to the children [the unfaithful Jews] and
> the disobedient [the unfaithful Jews] to the wisdom of the
> just [to the covenant fathers]. Luke 1:17

For what purpose?

To make ready a people prepared for the Lord (verse 17).

Did you catch that? Do you see now why God is going to send Elijah the prophet in these last days "to make ready a people [the Bride] prepared for the Lord."

In the transfiguration, Jesus reveals Himself walking in His kingdom with Moses and Elijah (read the account in Mark 9:1-10). Why Moses and Elijah? Why not Abraham, Isaac, and Jacob? What is that all about? Here is the reason:

Moses represents the law; he is the one God used to present the law (Torah) to His people. Elijah represents the prophets whom God used in the past and will use in the future to restore the law, bringing His people back to covenant relationship, preparing them to be the Bride of Christ.

Obviously, as you read the text about the transfiguration, the disciples of Jesus did not understand the meaning of Moses and Elijah together with Jesus. However, it is vital that we, as believers, understand the relationship.

In order for the Jews today to be saved and become a part of the Bride, they must turn their hearts to their Messiah, Christ (become Torah-observant believers in Christ). And in order for the Gentile believers in Christ (the organized church) to become a part of the Bride, they must turn their hearts to the Jews (covenant people) and become Torah-observant believers in Christ.

In order for all of this to happen, the prophets ("Elijah") must first come to restore to the organized church the knowledge and importance of living by the commandments of God (the Torah), which means walking in covenant relationship.

This restoration is what this book is all about. God is in the process of making a major shift in the organized church today to bring about the preparation of the Bride. Not all churches will embrace this truth. But Christ will have a Bride. It will be composed of Jew and Gentile believers, who are saved by faith in the blood of Jesus, living in covenant relationship, conforming to the very image of Christ, which means living righteously in accordance with the commandments of God (the Torah) and showing complete loyalty and adoration to the Father and to the Son.

MY STORY

We saw at the end of chapter 3 an amazing prophecy. God said that in the end time, He would bring about a sovereign move of the Holy Spirit (a restoration) where the "hearts of the fathers" (Jews) would turn toward the believers in Christ and the "hearts of the believers" (mainstream Christianity) would turn toward the fathers (Jews). We see this movement happening now. Many Jews today are giving their hearts to their Messiah, Jesus Christ, and becoming born again, yet remaining true to the commandments (the Torah) of God, while many evangelical, charismatic, and Pentecostal believers are turning their hearts to obey the commandments of God (the Torah), as they learn the roots of their Christian faith.

What must be understood is that the roots movement for the Christian believer is not about returning to the roots of Judaism (that is, learning the religion of the Jews and how they worshipped Jehovah God); rather, it is about returning to the "faith once delivered" (Jude 3), that is, returning to the written Torah, not the oral law that is based on tradition and is at the heart of Judaism. (See chapter 5 for an explanation of what *Torah* means.)

Now, when the subject of obedience to Torah or the law is brought up, right away, believers' thoughts tend to go in this direction: "Oh, that's legalism." Or "Jesus did away with the law at the cross." And the reason for this thinking is because that is what most mainstream Christians have been taught from the pulpit for years. The mind-set of the organized church today has been conditioned to believe that the law is for the Jews only and not for the believers in Christ.

I have been blessed in my Christian walk. I grew up as a youngster in a mainstream denominational church, yet like most teenagers, I drifted far away from God and did my own thing. Then in 1976, at the age of thirty, after living many years without God in my life, I was called into a conservative Christian fellowship, which was unique in this way: Its focus was on the kingdom of God and living by the laws of God.

For over twenty-two years in this fellowship, I kept the Sabbath Day, observed the seven Feasts of God, ate clean foods, and walked in covenant relationship with my Creator God. I never once believed that keeping the laws of God earned my salvation. I came to realize through my own intense Bible study that God, as my Creator, set in motion these spiritual laws (Torah) for my well-being (see Deut. 6:24). I learned that through living a life of obedience, I was being transformed into His image.

During this time, I was tremendously blessed. I met my wife and became a father of two beautiful girls. God blessed me with my own engineering firm, which became very successful. Yet I felt that something was missing in my relationship with God, the Father, and Jesus Christ, my Savior and King. Then in 1997, the Holy Spirit showed up in my life during a revival in Brownsville, Florida, which changed my life forever. You see, what was missing was a revelation and understanding of the role and purpose of the Holy Spirit in a believer's life.

God's Holy Spirit became real to me. I immersed myself in the charismatic movement, learned and grew in the gifts of the Spirit, was called into the fivefold ministry, became strong in warfare and deliverance, and operated under the apostolic and prophetic anointing. It was during this informative season of "training and equipping" that I drifted away from meeting on the Sabbath and keeping the feast days. Although I knew in my spirit that the Creator God designed His laws for man to live by for his good, I lost my first love for obeying all of His commandments. How did this happen? I bought into the deception of the enemy that, although God's laws were good and holy, they were only for the Jews to keep and not needed for Christians.

In early 2002, my wife and I started a ministry, called Triumphant Christian Center Church, with a desire to share with other believers how to live a life of victory. Within two months of our ministry, we came under severe attacks of the enemy, whereby my engineering firm was falsely accused of multiple unlawful practices, resulting in being sued for over $4 million. As a result of the lawsuits, I lost over $2 million in contracts and had to lay off almost all fifteen of my employees. It was during this time, by the grace of God, that we became involved with an apostolic and prophetic ministry. We learned quickly that when you are in a war, you need reinforcements. We did get the total victory over time (our name and good reputation was restored) and continued our public ministry.

In early 2006, I received a prophetic word from the Holy Spirit that God was going to take me back to my beginnings, where I first started my relationship with Him. I knew immediately what that meant. Before I received that word, God's Holy Spirit was leading me to go back to the holy days—the Sabbath and the feast days. With the comfort of the prophetic word, I began not only to study these days more deeply but to teach Torah to our flock. (I had regained my first love, praise God.)

We changed our services from Sunday to Saturday and began to keep the feast days for those who could get off from work. It was a hard transition for some of our flock, which led some to turn away. In addition to this, we never did fully recover from the effects of Hurricane Katrina, which occurred in 2005. We lost our church building in the storm, and 80 percent of our flock moved out of the area. With all of this happening, we believed God had another season for us. In early 2009, after seven years of ministering in a public forum, we made the decision (with God's help) to close our public ministry.

Now, at the time of this writing, we minister to other churches as God opens those doors.

TORAH

It has been interesting to teach in denominational and Pentecostal churches and to see how ambivalent many believers are concerning what they believe. For example, when teaching about God's Passover versus the traditional Easter, I ask the question: "How can you reconcile three days and three nights Jesus said He would be in the grave (proof of His Messiahship) against the day and a half of the traditional Good Friday night to Easter sunrise morning?" The typical response is, "Well, I've always wondered about that. I never understood how you can get three days out of one and a half days. But it doesn't matter to me how many days Jesus was in the grave. The main thing is that He was resurrected."

But the point is, it does matter. If you believe that Jesus was in the tomb a day and a half, and Jesus said the only sign he would give that he is the true Messiah would be the sign of Jonas, "for as [just like] Jonas was three days and three nights in the whale's belly; so shall the Son of man be three days and three nights in the heart of the earth" (Matt. 12:40), where does that leave your faith? Are you believing in a religion rather than in the true Word of God?

We, as Christians, have for so long been spoon-fed traditional dogma from the pulpit that we tend not to question doctrine, even though we can see in the Bible that what we are being taught doesn't agree with the Word.

This is what happens when the subject of Torah or obedience to God's law is taught. The mainstream teaching doesn't agree with the Word of God. For example, in Matthew 5:17, Jesus says:

> Think not that I am come to destroy the law, or the prophets: I am not come to destroy, but to fulfil [to preserve its true meaning].

Did you catch what Jesus was saying in this verse? He said, "Don't even think that I came to destroy the law." Jesus knew there would be an attack against keeping the commandments of God.

Yet it is taught today that Jesus did away with the law (destroyed the law) by "nailing it to the cross." It has been accepted as fact that when Jesus died on the cross, the law was done away with, that we are now under grace and not under the law, and that we, as Christians, are now to live under the "new covenant of love and grace" and not under the "old covenant of law."

It is not my intent to bash other ministries who hold to these beliefs. I sincerely desire that both pastors and believers will re-examine, take a fresh look at, what Jesus and the early apostles taught on the law (Torah) and on the new covenant relationship. As has been already discussed in the previous chapters, God puts a supreme emphasis on His people walking in obedience to His laws, statutes, and ordinances (His Torah) because through obedience to His Word (His written and living Word), we can experience a deep, intimate relationship with our Creator God and Savior Jesus Christ.

Let me give you an example of how obedience to God's laws brings you into a deeper relationship with Him. Not long after I began to keep the Sabbath Day holy (resting from worldly affairs and focusing on God's Word and His creation), I began to understand the Godhead as Creator of all things, natural and spiritual. God (who became Father) was the great Thinker, Planner, and Architect of the Universe ("Let us make …"). The Word (which later became Jesus Christ, the Son) brought forth the creation plan by speaking it into existence ("And God said …"). And God's Holy

Spirit was the power through which creation took place ("by the word of His power").

I began to understand how God, as Creator, designed laws in the natural and spiritual realm to assist mankind in life on this earth. For example, we live in an age where we have tapped into God's designed laws of physics, electricity, electro-magnetism, gravity, and thermodynamics to better our lives on earth. But God also designed spiritual laws (because man is spirit) and put them in motion for us to live by, to be conformed into the very image of God. These laws can be summarized in the Ten Commandments, which God gave to human beings as his gift of grace, to show us how to live the way of love: outflowing love toward God first and then toward our neighbor as ourselves. It is very important for the believer to understand that God, the Father, and Jesus Christ not only have love, they are Love (1 John 4:8). And for this reason, they gave mankind the laws of love (codified in the Ten Commandments) on how to live in right relationship with their Creator and with other human beings.

God also put into motion the law of sin and death, where when we sin (when we don't believe God or act contrary to His Word), we bring upon ourselves separation from our Creator, which (if not repented) brings death or total eternal separation from our Maker. When I pray today, I start with "Heavenly Father, great Creator God." If you want to get intimate with your heavenly Father, who gave you life, honor Him on the seventh day by resting, studying His Word, and enjoying His creation.

Remember: Being obedient does not mean being legalistic. Jesus obeyed His Father's commandments, leaving for us a great example to follow. Jesus came, not to live His life for us, but to live His life through us. Jesus obeyed the Ten Commandments, including keeping the Sabbath Day and also God's feast days. He obeyed the law of clean and unclean foods, and so did His apostles and the early church. He desires all of His people to obey Him. By obeying God's Word (which is based on love), we show that we love Him (John 14:15). By obeying God's Word, we show our allegiance to His kingdom. By obeying God's Word, we become one with Christ and with the Father. We become part of the Bride.

An All-Out Assault

From the very beginning, there has been an all-out assault against the church (the called-out ones) by Satan, the devil. Christ said this would happen. In Matthew 16:18, Jesus said: "I will build my church [*ekklesia*, the called-out ones] and the gates of hell shall not prevail against it." He knew Satan and his kingdom would try to destroy the children of God. The strategy of the enemy against the church is very sly and crafty. He very rarely uses a frontal attack. His best plan of attack is from within the church, using deception from false ministers. Jesus warned of this strategy. He says in Matthew 7:15, "Beware of false prophets, which come to you in sheep's clothing, but inwardly they are ravening wolves." Jesus gets more specific in Matt. 24:4-5; notice what He says would happen in the end time, the very generation we are living in now:

> "Take heed that no man deceive you. For many will come in my name [representing me] saying, I am Christ [saying, this is who Christ is and what he teaches] and shall deceive many."

Did you catch what Jesus was saying? He says to our generation today, "Take extreme care that no man deceive you." Why? Because deception is how the enemy works against God's people. Remember Eve? Jesus stated that many (not a few) in the church today, who claimed to represent Him (apostles, prophets, evangelists, pastors, and teachers), shall (not could) deceive many (not just a few). My friend, I am not claiming that ministers of the faith today purposely set out to deceive the flock. There is much false doctrine in the Christian church today that many have accepted because it was never tested against the true Word of God, only accepted by tradition. Do you have the courage to believe the truth?

Notice this warning from the apostle Paul, a warning that he gave to the elders of the church about thirty years after Christ's resurrection (Acts 20:28-32):

Take heed therefore unto yourselves, and to all the flock, over the which the Holy Ghost hath made you overseers, to feed the church of God, which he hath purchased with his own blood.

For I know this, that after my departing shall grievous wolves enter in among you, not sparing the flock.

Also of your own selves shall men arise, speaking perverse things, to draw away disciples after them.

Therefore watch, and remember, that by the space of three years I ceased not to warn every one night and day with tears.

And now, brethren, I commend you to God, and to the word of his grace [the Torah], which is able to build you up, and to give you an inheritance among all them which are sanctified.

Paul knew how the enemy worked. He knew the enemy would send evil men into the church with false doctrine to draw away (deceive) many of the sheep. This strategy of Satan happened then, and it has continued up until the present time. The greatest assault upon the church has been to perpetuate the false doctrine that either the law of God, which is based on love, has been done away with or that the commandments of God are for the Jews only and not for the New Testament church. By doing this, Satan has been able to convert the church of God into a lawless (without law) church. Notice what Paul says in verse 32. He says, "I commend you [brethren] to God and to the word of his grace." When Paul says "the word of his grace," he is speaking of the written word, called the Torah (I will explain later in detail the meaning of Torah). And Paul adds that the "word of grace" (Torah) is able to "build you up" (to make you strong so you won't be deceived) and "to give you an inheritance among all them which are sanctified" (to enable you to be in the kingdom of God, reaching your full reward).

Without Law

Now, I want you to notice what happens when the church becomes without law.

> Not every one that saith unto me, Lord, Lord, shall enter into the kingdom of heaven; but he that doeth the will of my Father which is in heaven.
>
> Many will say to me in that day, Lord, Lord, have we not prophesied in thy name? and in thy name have cast out devils? and in thy name done many wonderful works?
>
> And then will I profess unto them, I never knew you: depart from me, ye that work iniquity (Matt. 7:21-23).

Here is a passage of scripture most are familiar with, yet few understand its true meaning.

Here Jesus is speaking to those who are believers in Him. Paraphrasing, He says: "Not everyone who calls Me, Lord Lord, shall enter into my kingdom. Only the one who walks in obedience to the Father's will shall enter in." Do you know what the Father's will is? Please understand these verses and what Jesus is revealing here. He says in the Day of Judgment (on that day), which will take place in heaven, many believers will say to him (paraphrasing again), "Lord, haven't we prophesied in your name, and cast out demons in your name, and done many wonderful works in your name?" You get the sense here, by the nature of the response, that those saying "Lord Lord" did not receive the reward they thought they deserved. They thought they were doing the Father's will by prophesying, casting out demons, and doing many wonderful works. Then Jesus answers them. He says, "I profess (confess) to you; I never knew you [I never had an intimate relationship with you]: depart from me [leave my presence], ye that work iniquity" (you that are against obeying my law).

The word *iniquity* used by Jesus is Strong's word #458.

In the Greek, the word is *anomia*, where the *a* means "against" or "without," and *nomia* means "law"; therefore, the meaning is against the law.

Strong's Concordance defines *anomia* this way: "violation of the law, wickedness, iniquity, unrighteousness, transgression of the law." Anomia refers not to one living without law but to one who acts contrary to law.

Jesus knew exactly what He was saying and so did those who heard Him, particularly His disciples. Do we as believers today hear what Jesus is saying in this scripture? Are we living today contrary to the commandments of God, which means living contrary to the will of the Father?

It is vital to point out at this juncture a very profound distinction that seems to escape the Christian church today. When speaking about keeping the commandments or laws of God, great emphasis in the church is put on loving your neighbor by outreach programs, mission work, and evangelical campaigns. As good as these things are, and should be a part of Christian activity, notice where the emphasis should be, as told by our Savior and King, Jesus Christ, when He answers the question, "What is the great commandment in the Law?"

> You shall love the Lord your God [the Father] with all your heart, and with all your soul, and with all your mind. This is the first and great commandment (Matt. 22:37-38).

My dear friends, do you see what Jesus is saying? Our primary emphasis should be on loving God, the Father, pleasing Him by our obedience. As we love the Father, and honor Him with our obedience, we are loving Jesus and our neighbors, and the love of God is being perfected in us.

The apostle John understood this truth. Notice these powerful verses:

> Whoso keepeth his word [His commandments], in him [the believer] verily is the love of God perfected: hereby know we that we are in him. He that says he abideth

[continues] in him, ought himself also so to walk, even as he [Jesus] walked (1 John 2:5, 6).

Did you catch that? It says the love of God is perfected in the person who keeps His commandments. We are to walk as Jesus walked, being conformed into His image of love.

Now, before we go any further, I need to explain something from the previous passage (Matt. 7:21-23). Here is a profound nugget of truth. In this passage, Jesus tells those who are against His law to "depart from me." Here he is speaking about reward in heaven, not condemning believers to hell. The subject matter of these verses is "entering the kingdom of heaven," which is a reference to serving in the kingdom when Jesus returns.

The word *depart* is the Greek word *apochored* (Strong's #672). It is composed of two root words: *Apo* (#575), which denotes separation and departure, and *chored* (#5562), which always emphasizes the idea of separation or change of place. When putting these definitions together, the word *depart* means "to separate to a different place." What Jesus was saying here in verse 23 to those who discounted His law was this: "I never knew you [I never had an intimate relationship with you]; therefore, depart from me [go to a different place from those who honored and obeyed my Law]."

In other words, Jesus was letting it be known that those who are not keeping His Word, who are not walking as He walked, will not be with Him wherever He goes (which is the reward of the Bride) but will be separated to a different place, away from intimacy with Christ. Levels of reward are mentioned later on in this chapter, where Christ says some will be called "great" and some will be called "least" in the kingdom (or family) of God. Suffice to say at this part of the study, we need to realize that God gives rewards to His children. *Becoming the Bride is the greatest reward.*

As we go deeper into this study, we are going to see God's heart (His will), as He lays out in no uncertain terms the importance of living by His commandments (His Torah).

How God Works

What we need to realize at this juncture is that when God emphasizes obedience to His laws, He is *not* referring to our salvation. It is very important that we keep this point in mind as we go through this study. He is referring to covenant relationship (walking in obedience to His commandments), not salvation of the human soul. God's Word makes it very clear in Ephesians 2:8 that we are saved (born again) by His grace, through faith (in the blood of Jesus). No amount of keeping God's laws will save anyone.

What God shows us emphatically in His Word is that He has to get us saved *first*, and then He teaches us how to live the sanctified life by obeying His laws (the Torah). This is what He did with Israel. When the nation Israel did exactly what God said and put their faith in the "blood of the lamb," which was applied on the doorposts of their dwellings, God saved them from death (the death angel) and delivered them from slavery to sin (Egypt). Read the account in Exodus 12, 13, and 14.

After God saved Israel first, He then taught them how to live the sanctified life, a life separate from the world around them, a life based on the laws of God (the Torah). Notice how God approached the people of Israel at Mount Sinai. His first words to them were: "I am the LORD your God, which have brought you out of the land of Egypt [out of sin], out of the house of bondage" (Exod. 20:2). He was telling them, "I am the God who saved you from sin" (He saved them by His grace) and then He taught them how to conduct their lives righteously by giving them His commandments.

And God has dealt the same way with the believer. He has to get us saved first before we can understand and act on His Word because without salvation (being born again), God's Word is "foolishness" to the natural man (1 Cor. 2:14). This principle is pointed out by Jesus when speaking to Nicodemus (a Pharisee). The incident is recorded in John 3:3, where Jesus answers Nicodemus, "Verily, verily, I say unto you, Except a man be born again, he cannot see [know the things of] the kingdom of God."

Meaning of Torah

Now we need to know what the word *Torah* means. Normally, we refer to Torah as the first five books of the Old Testament. *Torah* is the Hebrew word translated into English as the word *law*. For example, in Exodus 16:4, the last part of the verse reads:

> that I [God] may prove them, whether
> they will walk in my law [Torah] or no.

Torah is Strong's word #8451. Strong's Concordance defines *Torah* this way:

> Torah signifies primarily direction, teaching, instruction (Prov. 13:14). It is derived from the verb Yarah, "to project, point out" (#3384) and hence to point out or teach the law of God is that which points out or indicates His will. It is not an arbitrary rule. Still less is it a subjective impulse; it is rather to be regarded as a course of guidance from above.

From the above meaning, we can see that *Torah* can be simply defined as teachings and instructions in how to live. I like how Apostle Paul said it in 2 Timothy 3:15-17:

> And that from a child thou hast known the holy scriptures, which are able to make thee wise unto salvation through faith which is in Christ Jesus.

> All scripture is given by inspiration of God, and is profitable for doctrine, for reproof, for correction, for instruction in righteousness:

> That the man of God may be perfect [mature], thoroughly furnished unto all good works.

We must remember that at the time Paul wrote this to Timothy, the "**holy scriptures**" and "**all scriptures**" referred to what we call today the Old

Testament or Hebrew text. In Hebrew thought, "Torah" is understood to mean the entire Old Testament, not just the Pentateuch (the first five books of the Bible).

Did you notice in verse 16 where Paul referred to "all scripture" as instruction in righteousness? Did you get that? That is what Torah is. (Please note: Every time the word *Torah* is used in this book, its meaning is "instruction in righteousness.") God lays out for us in His written Word (the Bible) detailed principles or instructions on how to live a life of righteousness. It is vital that we understand this principle about righteousness: We are saved by Christ's righteousness, but we are judged in this life (after salvation) by our own righteousness (how we live).

It is not the purpose of this book to do an exhaustive study on the Torah or to refute every teaching that speaks against the importance of living by the laws of God, which are based on love. I only ask the reader to keep a few things in mind:

We in the Western world tend to look at laws in a negative way. We look at laws as restricting or limiting freedom. And that is the mind-set we have when confronted with the knowledge of the laws of God. Jesus says, "You shall know the truth and the truth shall make you free" (John 8:32).

However, this scripture is used, by most, to justify the teaching that goes like this: "The truth is, that under the New Testament, we are under grace and not under the bondage of the law." This teaching leaves out the verse before it (verse 31), which says, "If you continue in my word, then are you my disciples indeed."

If we are continuing in the Word of God, we discover that the Word of God is truth (John 17:17). We discover that God's law is the truth (Ps. 119:142). We discover that all of God's commandments are truth (Ps. 119:151). This is what Jesus was referring to in John 8:32: "You shall know the truth [Torah] and the truth [Torah] shall make you free." Living by God's laws (instruction in righteousness) makes us free from sin. Remember that sin is "the transgression of the law" (1 John 3:4). It is sin that puts us in bondage, not God's law. Living by the spiritual laws of God puts a hedge of protection around us, guarding us from the evil one.

God cannot be separated from His Word. Jesus is the Word, the living Word. He changes not. In fact, He magnifies His Word above His name (Ps. 138:2). We get to know who God is through His Word. His law (His Torah) speaks of His character and His integrity. We get to know the Godhead intimately through obeying His written word, His Torah, His instruction in righteousness.

What about Animal Sacrifices?

Now, when we speak of the importance of conforming our lives to the authority of Torah, many will bring up this matter: "Well, what about those animal sacrifices and the harsh laws that demanded death, such as stoning those who committed adultery or broke the Sabbath or cursed their parents?"

We need to realize that many of the laws, judgments, and rituals that were carried out and practiced were relevant only when there was a tabernacle in the wilderness or a temple in Jerusalem. We see the example of Paul (many years after the death and resurrection of Jesus) observing the Laws of Purification before entering the temple (Acts 21:26). Yet all these temple practices as detailed in the Torah were discontinued in AD 70, when the Roman government destroyed the temple. As long as there was no temple in Jerusalem, these sacrificial laws and temple rituals were put on hold (not done away with) until Christ returns and the new temple is built in Jerusalem during the millennium (see Ezek., chapters 40-46).

Some may ask, "What about the 613 laws mentioned in the Torah?" Oddly enough, you are probably already keeping some of the laws mentioned in the Torah. For example: Love your neighbor as yourself (Lev. 19:18). Remember this: The laws given in the Torah were meant to govern a nation and include some laws that pertain to women only, the priesthood only, Levites only, men only, married people only, children only, and so on. Trust

God to show you in His law where you can make changes in your life, as you grow in grace and knowledge.

These changes will include, as a minimum, obeying the Ten Commandments, including keeping the Sabbath Day holy, observing God's seven annual feast days as mentioned in Leviticus 23 (see chapter 9), and eating clean foods, as discussed in Deuteronomy 14.

My friend, please understand this truth: The major restorational work God is doing in these last days is restoring the Torah (His instructions in righteousness) back into His church. The unveiling of the mystery of the Bride of Christ works hand in glove with the Torah's restoration.

You may be asking yourself, "What is so important about restoring the knowledge of God's laws [His Torah] back to His church [His called-out ones]?" It has everything to do with preparing the Bride for Christ. The Bride is to be conformed into the very image of Christ. Notice what the apostle Paul says in Romans 8:29:

> For whom he [the Father] did foreknow, he also did predestinate [predetermine] to be conformed to the image of his Son, that he [Jesus] might be the firstborn among many brethren.

How was this to happen? How was God, the Father, going to transform us into "the image of His Son"? The only way was for us to freely (of our own free will) give our life (die to self) and live according to the "instructions in righteousness" (God's Torah).

In order to understand the process of how the Father was going to transform us into His image, we need to understand that God created us as a spirit, having a soul (mind, intellect, personality), and living in a fleshly body. The apostle Paul makes this clear in 1 Thessalonians 5:23 when he writes:

> And the very God of peace sanctify you wholly; and I pray God your whole spirit and soul and body be preserved blameless unto the coming of our Lord Jesus Christ.

Romans 7:14 says "the law [Torah] is spiritual." God created His spiritual laws for us, who are spirits, to live by. God, who is Spirit, relates to us through our spirit and not through our flesh. Our fleshly carnal mind is "enmity against God." Paul writes about this in Romans 8:6-7:

> For to be carnally minded is death; but to be spiritually minded is life and peace. Because the carnal mind is enmity against God: for it is not subject to the law of God [the Torah], neither indeed can be.

To be "spiritually minded" requires us to be "born again," to receive another nature: God's nature, which is the work of the Holy Spirit within us.

For the Bride to be conformed into the very image of God requires those born-again believers, who are called, to walk as Jesus walked, to live by faith according to the spiritual laws God has set in motion for us to live by, that is, to live by the Torah (instructions in righteousness). It is by this process of being led by the Holy Spirit, walking by faith, living by the spiritual laws of God that transforms the spirit in us to the image of God. This is why it is important that God, through His Holy Spirit, is restoring Torah back into His church.

End of Torah?

Many will argue that when Christ came and died for the sins of the world, He did away with Torah. This belief comes from a misinterpretation of Romans 10:4. Let's analyze it. Romans 10:4 says:

> For Christ is the end of the law [Torah], for righteousness to everyone that believes.

The Greek word translated *end* in English is *telos* (Strong's word #5056), which is defined as follows: "to set out for a definite point or goal."

In other words, *telos* implies arrival at a goal or destination. Putting this meaning into verse 4, we read that "Christ is the goal or destination for which Torah points toward or reaches."

This is similar to what Paul says in Galatians 3:24:

> Wherefore the law [Torah] was our schoolmaster to bring us unto Christ.

Did you catch that? Christ is the destination, not the termination (end) of Torah. Remember: Jesus said He "came not to destroy the law [Torah]" (Matt. 5:17).

One of the primary purposes of Torah is to lead us to Christ, not only for salvation, but that we might become like Him, that we might become like-minded, because Torah is "instruction in righteousness." Torah leads us into obedience of God's commandments ("all [His] commandments are righteousness," Ps. 119:172). Without Torah, we would not know what sin is, for sin is the transgression of the law (Torah) (1 John 3:4).

What about Paul?

When discussing the importance of obeying the commandments of God, questions immediately arise about the teachings of Paul that seem to contradict the teachings of Jesus. Let me emphatically state that Paul's teachings in no way contradict the Word of God. In fact, when properly understood, Paul's teachings support and back up the Torah in every way. It is not the purpose of this book to examine scriptures written by Paul that appear to conflict. This point is sure: Paul was a devoted Pharisee who was faithful to the Torah and remained so until his death.

It must be remembered that in New Testament time, the Pharisees were the most influential group that held sway over the Jews. They not only had control over the synagogues, they had tremendous control over much of the people in Judea. By all accounts, the Pharisees "were responsible for the transformation of Judaism from a religion of sacrifice to one of law.

They were developers of the oral tradition, the teachers of the two-fold law: written and oral" (Holman Illustrated Bible Dictionary by Holman Bible Publishers, Trent C. Butler, General Editor, 2003, p. 917).

It was the Pharisees Jesus took issue with because they held to the oral law (a man-made commentary on the written law) as supreme over the written law of God, the Torah. Notice what Jesus told the Pharisees in Mark 7:7-9:

> Howbeit in vain do they [the Pharisees] worship me, teaching for doctrines the commandments of men [the oral law]. For laying aside the commandment of God, you hold the tradition of men, as the washing of pots and cups: and many other such like things you do … Full well you reject the commandment of God [written law], that you may keep your own tradition [oral law].

In Acts 24:14, Paul defends himself against his accusers, stating his commitment to God's law:

> But this I confess unto you, that after the way which they call heresy, so worship [serve] I the God of my fathers, believing all things which are written in the law [Torah] and in the prophets.

In Acts 23:1, Paul defends himself this way:

> Men and brethren, I have lived in all good conscience before God until this day.

Paul, in saying that he has "lived in all good conscience before God," was making the point that as a good Pharisee, he was living properly in accordance with the written laws of the Mosaic covenant. Notice verse 6. Paul says, "I am a Pharisee." Paul lived as a Pharisee, in complete obedience to God's written laws. He says, "Be you followers [imitators] of me, even as I also am of Christ" (1 Cor. 11:1).

Now notice again what Paul says passionately in Acts 24:14:

> But this I confess unto thee, that after the way [living
> by written Torah, not oral Torah] which they [Pharisee]
> call heresy, so worship [serve] I the God of my fathers,
> believing all things which are written in the law [Torah]
> and in the prophets.

Yes, some of what Paul wrote about is difficult to understand, but rest assured, his writings did not conflict with the sayings of Jesus.

Notice what Peter wrote in 2 Peter 3:16:

> As also in all his [Paul's] epistles, speaking in them of these
> things; in which are some things hard to be understood,
> which they that are unlearned and unstable wrest, as they
> do also the other scriptures, unto their own destruction.

Remember: early translators of New Testament scriptures were Gentiles and knew little or nothing of true Jewish ideas and thoughts (they were "unlearned and unstable"). This allowed for personal bias to enter into translations and thus caused much of the confusion we see today, particularly when it involves the letters written by Paul.

For those of you who want to go deeper in understanding personal bias in the translations of Paul's letters, I highly recommend the following book: *Galations: A Torah-Based Commentary in First-Century Hebraic Context,* by Avi Ben Mordechai.

As I close out this chapter on the importance of living by the commandments of God (the Torah), I want to leave you with several thoughts. One is that the law (Torah) is very special to God. It was very special to Jesus as He walked this earth two thousand years ago. Why? Because the law (the Torah) came from the Father, the lawgiver, who judges everyone's work of obedience during their time on earth (see 1 Pet. 1:17).

Jesus obeyed the Father in everything. He was loyal to His Father. He yielded up His will to do the Father's will, and it pleased His Father ("you are my beloved son, in whom I am well pleased," Mark 1:11).

You see, Jesus understood the power of obedience. Paul wrote about it in Romans 6:16:

> Know ye not [Don't you know], that to whom you yield yourselves servants to obey, his servants you are to whom you obey; whether of sin unto death, or of obedience unto righteousness?

Jesus knew that the law (Torah) was spiritual (Rom. 7:14), and that by living in harmony with the law of God, our spirit would be conformed into the very image of God Himself, developing in righteous character. Notice what the apostle Peter wrote in 1 Peter 1:22-23:

> Seeing you have purified your souls in obeying the truth [the Torah] through the [Holy] Spirit unto unfeigned love of the brethren … being born again, not of corruptible seed, but of incorruptible, by the Word of God, which lives and abides for ever.

Did you catch what Peter was saying? We become born again (purify our souls), by obeying the truth, by living by the Word of God. Remember that Jesus said, "It is written [in Deut. 8:3], That man shall not live by bread alone, but by every word [that proceeds out of the mouth] of God" (Luke 4:4).

Christ not only lived by the laws of God, He also taught them and magnified them to His disciples (see Matt. 5:17-37). He stated in Matthew 5:19 that the person who not only obeyed the law (the Torah), but also taught others to keep it, would be called great in the kingdom of God. That is a reference to the Bride, who will be called great in the kingdom. Why? Because while on earth "in training for reigning," this special group (the Bride) lives by the commandments of God, walks as Jesus walked in complete obedience, and teaches others to do so also. It will be because of their preparation and commitment to the laws of God (walking in covenant relationship) that Christ knows His Bride will be faithful and totally loyal to His Word for all eternity.

Now, did you notice the first part of Matthew 5:19? Christ said, "Whosoever therefore shall break one of these least commandments and shall teach men so, he shall be called the least in the Kingdom of Heaven." There will be many who will be "weeping and gnashing of teeth" because they fell to the deception of the enemy and believed that the law (the commandments of God) did not apply to them. Consequently, they will lose their reward of Kingship and being a part of the Bride of Christ. (They will be guests at the wedding, but not part of the Bride.) They will be called "least" in the kingdom—not "great." Why? Because Jesus Christ will not be unequally yoked to a Bride who willingly broke the commandments of God and taught others to break them also.

As a side note, it must be remembered that during the millennium, the thousand-year rule and reign of Christ, the Bride will be teaching the nations about the commandments of God and how they are to live by them. How can you teach the Torah in the millennium if you have not embraced and lived by the Torah during your lifetime here on earth?

Jesus, in Revelation 3:9, when speaking to the church of Philadelphia (who represents the Bride—see chapter 8), makes a powerful statement to those believers who have bought into Satan's lie and deception that the law has been done away with and is not applicable for the church today. He calls these believers "the synagogue of Satan, who say they are Jews [God's chosen people] but are not, but do lie."

Remember: This is a message to God's church, born-again believers, but who are deceived. Those are strong words used by Jesus, yet He makes His point about whose camp those believers are in. Now, notice what follows. Christ says, "Behold, I will make them [of the synagogue of Satan [my people, yet deceived] to come and worship before your [the Bride's] feet [this event will most likely occur in heaven], and to know that I have loved you" ["because you have kept my word and not denied my name"].

The apostle John understood what separated those believers who had an intimate relationship with Christ from those who had not, yet thought they did. Notice his very powerful words in 1 John 2:2-6, with my commentary added in brackets:

> And hereby we do know that we know [have an intimate relationship with] him, if we keep his commandments.
>
> He that says, I know him [intimately] and keeps not his commandments, is a liar, and the truth [about keeping God's commandments] is not in him [he is of the synagogue of Satan, Rev. 3:9).
>
> But whoso keeps His word [his commandments], in him verily is the love of God perfected [Jesus says, "If you love me keep my commandments," John 14:15].
>
> He that says he abideth [dwells] in him [Chris] ought himself also so to walk, even as he [Jesus] walked [in total obedience].

The Bible, from Genesis through Revelation, cries out to us about the importance of obeying the Word of God, for it brings transformation, relationship, and reward. Notice what it says in the last book (Revelation), the last chapter (chapter 22), and verse 14:

> Blessed are they that do his commandments [Torah], that they may have right to the tree of life, and may enter in through the gates into the city [Holy Jerusalem].

That sums it up pretty well, doesn't it?

THE TORAH WITHIN US

After hitting hard in the last chapter about the importance of Christians living by the commandments of God (instruction in righteousness), I am compelled to add this chapter about the Torah within us.

There will be some of you reading this book who, at this juncture, may be turned off by how firmly I make this point about obedience. This is because we have been so conditioned in our thinking to believe that we cannot keep the commandments, and that is why Jesus came to keep them for us. This thinking has led Christians to believe that they are under a curse if they try to live by the law. After all, doesn't the Bible say that "Christ has redeemed us from the curse of the law" (Gal. 3:13)?

My friend, if you fall into this category, I understand. I ask that you stay with me as I go through this chapter on the Torah within us. I believe it will clear up any confusion you may have about the importance of walking a life of obedience to the laws of God.

First, let me address the scripture quoted above (Gal. 3:13). Christ has indeed redeemed us from the curse of the law. But we need to ask ourselves, what exactly is the curse of the law? The Bible tells us that the curse of the law is sin and death. It is from sin and death that Christ has redeemed us. "The wages of sin is death" (Rom. 6:23). It must be understood that the law is not a curse. Romans 7:12 says: "The law is holy, and the commandment holy, and just and good." Now notice what follows in verse 13: "Was then that which is good [the law] made [to bring] death unto me? God forbid."

Paul goes on to say that it was sin (not the law) that was working death in him by using the law, which reveals sin. Remember what sin is? "Sin is the transgression of the law" (1 John 3:4). Do you see now what Paul was referring to in Galatians 3:13: "Christ has redeemed us from the curse of the law [which is sin and death]"?

Now to understand the Torah within us is to understand what takes place under the New Covenant and why it was necessary for God to upgrade the Sinai covenant (old covenant).

It was God's intent that Israel, who had entered into the Sinai covenant to be Jehovah God's covenant people, would be separate from all the nations:

> And you [Israel] shall be holy [separate and dedicated] unto me; for I the LORD am holy [separate], and have severed you [set you apart] from other people, that you should be mine (Lev. 20:26).

Also, it was God's intent that the nations would learn from them. Notice these encouraging words of Moses to the nation Israel just before they were to go into the promised land:

> Behold, I have taught you statutes and judgments, even as the LORD my God commanded me, that you should do so in the land whither you go to possess it. Keep therefore and do them; for this is your wisdom and your understanding in the sight of the nations, which shall hear all these statutes, and say, Surely this great nation is a wise and understanding people. For what nation is there so great, that hath statutes and judgments so righteous as all this law [Torah], which is set before you this day? (Deut. 4:5-7)

Yet, Israel failed to be that "shining light in a dark place." Why? Very simply, the people of Israel had a heart problem.

God knew this. Notice what He says in Deuteronomy 5:29:

> O that there were such an heart in them, that they would fear me, and keep all my commandments always.

But God never gave up on His plan and purpose for Israel. For He prophesizes to Ezekiel that in the end times, when His kingdom will be set up on the earth, He will gather the remnant of His people Israel and bring them back to the land of their inheritance, the promised land of Israel:

> For I [Jehovah God] will take you from among the heathen, and gather you out of all countries, and will bring you into your own land. A new heart also will I give you, and a new spirit will I put within you: and I will take away the stony heart out of your flesh, and I will give you an heart of flesh. And I will put my spirit within you, and cause you to walk in my statutes, and you shall keep my judgments, and do them (Ezek. 36:24, 26-27).

Did you notice what God said? He would give Israel (His people) a new heart, which could receive His Holy Spirit, enabling His people to obey and walk in covenant relationship.

Why is all this important? You see, under the old covenant, there was not the promise of a heart change, which required a move of the Holy Spirit to put the "laws into their minds and write them in their hearts" (Heb. 8:10). A heart change became available under the new (renewed) covenant after the death and resurrection of Jesus Christ, when the Father released His Holy Spirit into all the earth.

When we become born again as believers in Jesus Christ and in His shed blood, we become new creations in Christ. We are not the same. Something new has happened to us. We receive a new heart. Notice:

> Now he which stablisheth us with you in Christ, and hath
> anointed us, is God Who hath also sealed us, and given
> the earnest of the Spirit in our hearts (2 Cor. 1:21-22).

What has happened to us is that God the Father has placed within us
(within our spirit) His Holy Spirit, which brings about a heart change.

> But he that is joined unto the Lord is one spirit (1 Cor. 6:17).

When we receive God's Holy Spirit within us, we become one with him.
Our spirit is joined with His Spirit, and we become one. We are now a
new creation in Christ.

> After those days [after Christ was born, crucified, and
> raised from the dead], saith the Lord; I will put my laws
> into their mind, and write them in their hearts [in their
> spirits]: and I will be to them a God, and they shall be to
> me a people (Heb. 8:10).

What makes us a new creation is that God does something new with our
hearts.

To understand this new creation is to understand the new covenant. Many
do not realize that the covenant we are now under is a renewed covenant,
not a new covenant, as if it were brand new, never to have existed before.

The Greek word for *new* in Hebrews 8:8 is Strong's word #2537 (*kainos*),
which means:

> That which is unaccustomed or unused, not "new" in
> time, recent, but "new" as to form or quality, of different
> nature from what is contrasted as old.

In other words, *kainos* is describing something new and different, not in
the sense that something had never existed before, but that it had been
made better, renewed to a better condition.

Say, for example, you have a 1957 Chevy (a classic car), and you refurbish it with new seats, interior, paint job, and engine. You took something which existed (an old Chevy) and made it better. In others words, you renewed it. This is what God did with the covenant He gave Israel at Mount Sinai. He took the existing covenant (the Mosaic covenant, which was built upon the Abrahamic covenant) and made it better (the renewed covenant), because it was "established upon better promises," which included spiritual promises, such as the promise of eternal life.

Now notice Hebrews 8:7-10:

> For if the first covenant [Mosaic Covenant] had been faultless [unchangeable], then should no place have been sought for the second. For finding fault [blame] with them [the people, not the laws of the covenant], he saith, behold, the days come saith the Lord, when I will make a new [renewed] covenant with the House of Israel and with the House of Judah [my called-out people]: not according to the covenant that I made with their fathers in the day when I took them by the hand to lead them out of the land of Egypt; because they continued not in my covenant; and I regarded them not, saith the Lord. For this is the covenant that I will make with the House of Israel [my special called-out people] after those days, saith the Lord; I will put my laws into their mind, and write them in their hearts [in their spirit]: and I will be to them a God, and they shall be to me a people [a special called-out people—the church].

Did you catch what God was saying in these verses? The problem was not the covenant. The problem was with the people. They did not have a heart to obey. They did not have the Holy Spirit. So under the renewed covenant, which has better promises, God is going to change hearts upon conversion, upon accepting, by faith, Jesus Christ as Lord and Savior.

Now believers, upon repentance and faith in the blood of the Redeemer, will receive the Holy Spirit, which will enable them to live righteous lives. But it will be their choice to believe God's Word and to live by it.

God is not going to destroy His law (the Torah) under the new covenant. Rather, He is going to put His laws (His Torah) within the spirit of believers as they walk out in covenant relationship. Praise God.

As a side note, it must be understood what a covenant is and is not. In a spiritual sense, a covenant is not a contract. A covenant is a commitment: a commitment to a continuing relationship with our Creator. Whereas a contract is limited by time (having a beginning and an end), a covenant has only a beginning and lasts forever.

This is what the covenant with God is all about. It is a commitment to a continuing loving relationship with our Creator God forever. It began with Abraham, was enlarged with Moses, and was improved with better promises through Jesus Christ, the Messenger of the Covenant (Mal. 3:1).

Under the new (renewed) covenant, God is doing a work from the inside out—a heart change, putting the Torah within us. Our part is to begin living the new covenant by faith, walking in obedience, developing a continuing committed relationship with our heavenly Father and Jesus Christ forever.

THE TEN VIRGINS

We are going to see in this and in the following chapters that God has a lot to say about the Bride of Christ, about who they are, and what makes them different. Yet the Bride is hidden in scriptures, and it is up to us, guided by the Holy Spirit, to discern where and by what terms the Bride is identified. For example, we will find the Bride within the parable of the ten virgins. And not only that, but contained within the parable of the ten virgins are profound nuggets of truth that will "make you free."

The parable is found in Matthew 25:1-13. Now as we go through these verses, we are going to let the Bible interpret its own symbols. Many have gone astray in understanding this parable, letting their own biases explain the terms, rather than letting the Bible interpret itself. So let's begin, going verse by verse, line upon line.

> Then shall the kingdom of heaven be likened unto ten virgins, which took their lamps, and went forth to meet the bridegroom.

In verse 1, the setting is the kingdom of heaven (the soon-coming government of God) and who will be in it. The subject matter is about virgins. Who are the virgins? In 2 Corinthians 11:2, we find the answer:

> For I am jealous over you with godly jealousy: for I have
> espoused you to one husband that I may present you as a
> chaste virgin to Christ.

Paul is speaking to the church (believers) "as a chaste virgin." What does the term *lamp* represent? Psalm 119:105 says "your word is a lamp unto my feet." Here we see that "lamp" represents the "Word of God," which is a reference to the written Word of God, or Torah (instruction in righteousness). Who is the Bridegroom? Without making a broad leap, we can confidently say this represents Jesus Christ (remember that the setting is about the kingdom of God).

So we begin to see in verse 1 that Jesus is telling a parable about the called-out ones (the church), which He likens to ten virgins. It is interesting to note here that Jesus uses the number ten, which can represent "testing." For example, in Luke 19:13-25, we read about one of Jesus's parables where ten servants are called to see what they would do when given the same amount of money. In other words, it was a parable about testing. In the parable about the ten virgins, could Jesus be referring to the corporate body of the church, which has been called to a life of testing? I believe this is the case.

The last part of verse 1 says, "and went forth to meet the bridegroom." Could this be a reference to the Bride getting herself ready to meet the Bridegroom when He comes?

In verse 2, Jesus says:

> And five of them were wise and five were foolish.

Who are the "wise" and who are the "foolish"? What distinguishes the wise from the foolish? Jesus gives the answer in Matthew 7:24, 26:

> Whosoever heareth these sayings of mine and doeth them,
> I will liken him unto a wise man.

When you see a verb having an "eth" on the end of it, like "heareth" and "doeth," it means "a continuing action." In other words, what Jesus is saying here in this verse is that "whoever continues to hear my words and continues to walk in obedience to them, I will liken him to a wise man."

> And every one that heareth these sayings of mine, and doeth them not, shall be likened unto a foolish man.

Here, Jesus makes a very clear statement when He says that "everyone who continues to hear my words and continues to disobey me, I will consider him a foolish man."

Continuing in the parable, verse 3 and 4 say:

> They that were foolish took their lamps, and took no [extra] oil with them: But the wise took [extra] oil in their vessels with their lamps.

In these verses, we begin to see a wider distinction between the wise and the foolish. The oil represents the Holy Spirit (see Luke 4:18 for the connection between the Holy Spirit and the anointing with oil), which brings illumination (revelation and understanding) to the Word of God. The wise (those who obey the commandments of God) had an extra measure of oil in their lamps. Why was this the case? Where did this extra oil come from?

God, in His Word, tells us that He gives His Holy Spirit (oil) to those who obey Him (Acts 5:32), and He gives a good understanding to all those who keep His commandments (Ps. 111:10). So we begin to see what sets the wise apart from the foolish. The wise made themselves ready (prepared themselves to meet the Bridegroom) by obeying the Word of God, which led them to have more of an anointing (representing more oil) upon their lives to understand the Word of God, to grow in grace and in knowledge, and to have the faith to walk in obedience to His commandments. However, the foolish had limited understanding of the Word, represented by not having extra oil with their lamps.

We see in verses 5 and 6 that while the bridegroom was delayed, the virgins "slumbered and slept," and then the "cry was made" at midnight that the bridegroom was coming and it was time to go out and meet him. In other words, what was prophesied (in the Word of God, the Bible) to take place is now happening.

Now notice verse 7. It says, "Then all those virgins arose and trimmed their lamps." The "cry" went forth, and all the believers checked their Bibles to see if it were so. Verse 8 tells about the condition of the foolish. They had limited knowledge and were unprepared. "Give us of your oil [or understanding]." "How do you know it's time? We're not ready."

Notice the wise virgins' response in verse 9: "We can't give you what we have [which is our faith and understanding]. Our faith and understanding came at the high price of obedience." Remember what is written about Christ in Hebrews 5:8: He learned "obedience by the things which he suffered."

Then we see where the wise give the foolish good advice: "Go to those that have the truth and learn the way of obedience."

Are you beginning to see and understand how the Bride made herself ready?

Verse 10 gives the outcome: "And while they [the five foolish virgins] went to buy, the bridegroom came, and they that were ready [the five wise virgins] went in with him to the marriage: and the door was shut.

Many believers have a hard time in seeing this parable is about the church as a whole. How could God shut out a believer from the kingdom? What we need to realize is that the parable of the ten virgins is about reward (which is earned) and not about salvation (which is by faith). It is about those believers (the five wise virgins) who made themselves ready to be the Bride. The five foolish virgins represent believers who missed out on the reward of the Bride.

Serving in the kingdom of God, ruling and reigning with Jesus Christ, is reserved for the Bride. It is the highest reward given to redeemed person.

It is a reward reserved for the few, not for the many. Jesus mentions this truth in Luke 13:24-30, which is a corollary to Matthew 25:1-13:

> Strive to enter in at the strait gate: for many, I say unto you, will seek to enter in, and shall not be able.

> When once the master of the house is risen up, and hath shut to the door, and ye begin to stand without, and to knock at the door, saying, Lord, Lord, open unto us; and he shall answer and say unto you, I know you not whence ye are:

> Then shall ye begin to say, we have eaten and drunk in thy presence, and thou hast taught in our streets.

> But he shall say, I tell you, I know you not whence ye are; depart from me, all ye workers of iniquity.

> There shall be weeping and gnashing of teeth, when ye shall see Abraham, and Isaac, and Jacob, and all the prophets, in the kingdom of God, and you yourselves thrust out.

> And they shall come from the east, and from the west, and from the north, and from the south, and shall sit down in the kingdom of God.

> And, behold, there are last which shall be first, and there are first which shall be last.

Jesus made these remarks when He was asked, "Are there few that be saved?" (verse 23).

In His response, Jesus changes the focus from salvation to entering into His kingdom. Notice the language He uses in verse 24:

> Strive to enter in [into the kingdom] at the strait gate:
> for many, I say unto you, will seek to enter in [into my
> kingdom], and shall not be able.

Remember that "entering into the kingdom of God" refers to God's royal kingdom on earth during the thousand-year reign of Jesus Christ, where His Bride will be ruling and reigning with Him. Here, in verse 24, Jesus is speaking about reward, not salvation. Notice He says, "strive [fight against Satan] to enter in." It will be a fight of faith to hang on and walk the walk when the going gets tough. Remember: Salvation is by "grace through faith … not of works, lest any man should boast" (Eph. 2:8-9). However, reward is by overcoming (getting the victory) over the "wiles of the devil" (Eph. 6:11).

Jesus is giving a nugget of truth here in this verse that many believers do not fully understand. He says "strive to enter in at the strait gate." The word *strait* is Strong's #4728, which has the meaning of "narrow (from obstacles standing close about)." In other words, "strait gate" represents a life of encountering obstacles, which bring about anguish and distress, or as Strong defines it, as a life that "runs counter to natural inclinations."

In Matthew 7:13-14, Jesus says:

> Enter ye in at the strait gate: for wide is the gate, and broad
> is the way, that leadeth to destruction, and many there be
> which go in thereat: because strait is the gate, and narrow
> is the way, which leadeth unto life, and few there be that
> find it.

Again, the strait gate Jesus is speaking about is living a life of faith in the Word of God, a life which can be filled with anguish, distress, and suffering due to circumstances of life brought on by the enemy, Satan, the devil. Yet here, Jesus adds another element by saying, "and narrow is the way." What did He mean by that expression? The word *narrow* is Strong's #2346, which means "afflict, trouble, suffer tribulation."

Jesus said these things because he knew where the fight was going to be. The apostle Paul wrote about it in Ephesians 6:12:

"For we wrestle [fight] not against flesh and blood, but against principalities, against powers, against the rulers of the darkness of this world, against spiritual wickedness in high places [Satan's kingdom]."

Walking in covenant relationship with your Maker is not an easy life to live, and many will be unable to do so ("few there be that find it"). The reason for this is because of Satan and his kingdom who want to "kill, steal, and destroy" (John 10:10) the destiny of every born-again believer, especially those striving to enter in at the strait gate.

The apostle Paul understood about living the straight and narrow way, a life of tribulation and suffering. Look at what he went through: He received beatings five times, with thirty-nine stripes by his own people, the Jews; three times he was beaten with rods; once he was stoned (and probably died and brought back to life); he was shipwrecked three times, one time spent twenty-four hours in the sea.

While he journeyed, preaching the gospel of the kingdom of God, Paul faced danger in the sea, danger from robbers, danger from his own countrymen, danger from wild animals, even danger from false brethren in the church (2 Cor. 11:23-26). Yet, amidst all of these perils, Paul says at the end of his life:

> I have fought a good fight [against Satan and his kingdom]. I have finished my course. I have kept the faith. Henceforth, there is laid up for me a crown of righteousness [his reward], which the Lord, the righteous judge, shall give me at that day [when rewards are given]: and not to me only, but unto all them also that love his appearing (2 Tim. 4:7-8).

Paul knew who his enemy was because he wrote about it in 2 Cor. 12:7, where he said, "There was given to me a thorn in the flesh, the messenger [an evil angel] of Satan to buffet [strike] me." Paul knew all too well who wanted to destroy his destiny of becoming a part of the Bride (Eph. 6:12). He fought the enemy and won, knowing who he was in Christ and knowing the victory won for him (and all believers) at the cross. (See chapter 12 for more information on how to defeat the devil in your life.)

I'm not making the case that all the Bride must go through what Paul went through. The point is, there is a price to pay for living the sanctified (set apart) life in Christ Jesus. There is a price to pay to be in the royal kingdom of God. (Read Christ's words in Luke 14:26-33 on what it takes to be his discipline ones.) In Acts 14:22, we read, "We [born-again believers] must through much tribulation enter into the kingdom of God." That's what it means to strive to enter in at the strait gate.

Again, Jesus said in Matthew 7:13-14, "Enter ye in at the strait gate: for wide is the gate, and broad is the way, that leadeth to destruction, and many there be which go in thereat: because strait [suffering due to circumstances] is the gate, and narrow [trouble, tribulation] is the way, which leadeth unto life [eternal God life], and few there be that find it."

Jesus sums it up perfectly in Revelation 3:21:

> To him [or her] that overcometh [who overcomes tribulations and gets the victory over the enemy in this life] will I grant to sit with me in my throne [being my Bride]; even as I also overcame [overcame much tribulations and got the victory over Satan, the devil] and am set down with my Father in his throne.

Returning to Luke 13:25, which is a corollary to Matthew 25:10-12, Jesus mentions the "master" shutting the door on believers who knock to get in, saying, "Lord, Lord, open unto us." (Remember that the door was shut on reward, not salvation.) His response is almost identical to the one given in Matthew 25: "I know you not whence ye are" [I don't know where you are from]. The point Jesus is making is that there is no intimate relationship here due to how the believer lived, walking the wide and broad way.

Notice the response of those who were not able (willing) to enter in as God desired (verse 26):

> Then shall ye begin to say, We have eaten and drunk in thy presence, and thou hast taught in our streets.

Their response was, "Lord, we have spent time in your presence, eating and drinking [soaking in the Holy Spirit], learning of your Spirit." Their belief was that by spending time "in His presence," they were growing in their relationship with Jesus Christ. But notice what Jesus said in verse 27:

> But he [the Master] shall say, I tell you, I know you not whence ye are; depart from me, all ye workers of iniquity.

My dear brethren: I know it is hard to believe that spending time in God's presence does not equate to growing in intimacy with Jesus Christ. Spending time in His presence, where there is a tangible manifestation of the Father's Holy Spirit, where people are healed and set free, is an expression of the Father's love toward His people. Where the anointing of the Holy Spirit is working, yokes of bondages are broken, miracles occur, peoples' lives are changed forever. This is all about God showing love and mercy toward His creation. But it does not produce an intimate relationship. Remember that Jesus said, "If you love me, keep my commandments" [walk in obedience], not "If you love me, spend time in my presence."

The word *iniquity* in verse 27 is Strong's #93, which means "unrighteousness" or "lawlessness." Are you beginning to see and understand what Jesus is saying? An intimate relationship with Jesus Christ is based upon obedience to His Word, to His commandments ("If you love me, keep my commandments," John 14:15). Jesus is not going to marry a Bride who is not like-minded as He. Jesus loved the Father and obeyed everything He said. Notice Jesus's mind-set when He said, "For I came down from heaven, not to do mine own will, but the will of him that sent me" (John 6:38).

There will be great disappointment when many believers find out that they have been led astray in their belief system and have denied the true Word of God, missing out on their full potential. This is brought out in Luke 13:28:

> There shall be weeping and gnashing of teeth, when ye
> shall see Abraham, and Isaac, and Jacob, and all the
> prophets, in the kingdom of God, and you [workers of
> iniquity, against the law] yourselves thrust out [away from
> the presence of Christ, not condemned to hell].

My dear friends, did you see in the above verse whom Jesus said would be in His kingdom, who would be His Bride? Abraham, Isaac, Jacob, and all the prophets. Do you see the common denominator that connects all of these? It is this: They all walked in covenant relationship. They all lived by God's instruction in righteousness, following His commandments.

It is for this reason that I am writing this book about the mystery of the Bride. My heart aches for those who have been misled and will miss their destiny. Hear the heart of God in Revelation 18:4, where He pleads with His people:

> Come out of her [Babylon], my people, that you be not
> partakers of her sins.

"Babylon" is religious confusion and deception that the enemy, Satan, has brought into the church. The enemy has blinded the church in the understanding of covenant relationship and the importance of living by the laws of God. Remember: Sin is the breaking of God's laws (1 John 3:4). The church is confused and deceived when it holds to the belief that the law of God is no longer applicable to the believer. God's law has not been done away with but is intended for us to live by ("Man does not live by bread alone, but by every word that proceeds out of the mouth of God," Matt. 4:4).

As an aside, it must be understood that God does not have two people: the Jews and the church (meaning there are different paths of salvation for each). The Bible is very clear that God has one people made up of Jews and Gentiles, living under one covenant, the new (renewed) covenant. Jesus's "body" is not divided. He has one body: the called-out ones, Israel. The church is spiritual Israel, God's called-out ones. There is so much confusion about this point that it has led to the establishment of two major theological belief systems in the church today: replacement theology and dispensational theology. It is not the purpose of this book to discuss these two belief systems. I will leave it up to the reader to research them. The main point is that these theologies are a lie from the pit of hell, deceiving the church into either legalism or antinomianism.

There is another nugget of truth that has been lost on the Christian world, and it is found at the very beginning of God's Word, the Bible, in Genesis chapter 2. It has to do with the two trees planted in the garden of Eden: the tree of life and the tree of the knowledge of good and evil.

The tree of life represents living a God-centered way of life, living by His law of love, by His instruction in righteousness. The Bride (the five wise virgins) chose the tree of life. The tree of the knowledge of good and evil represents living a self-centered way of life, where you decide what is good and evil (under the influence of Satan), which has translated into the Christian life as deciding for yourself what is the best way to live, rather than listening to God's Word. In other words, it is the way of the five foolish virgins.

From the very beginning, it was God's desire, as Creator, for His greatest creation, man, to take of the tree of life, to walk in obedience to His laws and commandments, which are based on love—love toward God first and love toward others (Matt. 22:37-40). Now, in these last days, God, the Father, is preparing a Bride for His Son, Jesus. It will be the Bride who has chosen the tree of life. Which tree do you choose?

FIRSTFRUITS

In chapter 7, I made the comment that the Bride is hidden in scriptures, and I brought out how the parable of the ten virgins points directly to the Bride by the five wise virgins. Another term used in scripture which refers to the Bride is the "firstfruits." Before looking at a few familiar verses and pulling out rich nuggets of truth, we need to start at a place unfamiliar to most Christians today. That place is Leviticus 23, where God lays out His plan of salvation for mankind in His special days called feasts. To understand these feast days, we need to remember a simple principle of biblical interpretation, which goes something like this: The Old Testament is the New Testament concealed; the New Testament is the Old Testament revealed.

We can understand God's feast days by looking at the New Testament. For example, in Leviticus 23:4-5, God tells us that His first feast day is Passover. Jesus Christ is our Passover Lamb (1 Cor. 5:7). Just as faith in the lamb's blood saved the people of Israel from death, it is by faith in the blood of Jesus that we are saved from death. As we have covered before, the first thing God has to do for His people is to get us saved; we need to be born again and receive His Spirit so that we can obey Him. Thus, Passover pictures becoming born again, saved by faith in the blood of Jesus.

The next part of God's plan after we are born again is to teach us how to live the sanctified life, removing leavening from our lives, which represents sin, and living by unleavened bread, which represents righteousness. (Paul makes the analogy of leaven with sin and unleaven with righteousness in 1 Cor. 5:6-7.) This is expressed by God's second feast, called the Feast of Unleavened Bread. The people were instructed to remove all leavening products from their house, which symbolizes getting sin out of one's life.

Next, they were commanded to eat unleavened bread for seven straight days, symbolizing putting in righteousness or living a holy (sanctified) life. The period of seven days is significant because it represents completeness or perfection.

Now notice the next part of God's plan of salvation, after instructing His people to live righteously. The next feast that God commands His people to keep highlights a special group. Are you ready for this? The day is reckoned fifty days from the day the wave sheaf offering is held, during the days of Unleavened Bread. Please read Leviticus 23:15-17. Here, in these verses, we see that after the fifty days are determined, a special grain offering is presented, which is called "the firstfruits unto the LORD." This third feast of God's is called the Feast of Firstfruits. In Exodus 34:22, we also see this called the Feast of Weeks. In Numbers 28:26, this feast is referred to as "the Day of Firstfruits."

In the New Testament, this feast is called "the day of Pentecost" (Acts 2:1). The term *Pentecost* means "count fifty," which refers back to the instructions God gave the nation Israel in Leviticus 23:15-16, where fifty days are counted as explained above. It was on this day, the Feast of Firstfruits, that God introduced to His apostles the empowerment of His Holy Spirit and began calling out His church, from which comes His special group, His "firstfruits." The two loaves of bread mentioned in Leviticus 23:17, referred to as the "firstfruits," symbolize both Jews (Israel) and Gentiles making up the firstfruits.

It is interesting to note that it was on the Day of Firstfruits that God appeared on Mount Sinai and gave His law to His people, beginning the process on a national level of calling out a special group, who would obey His laws and walk in covenant relationship.

My friend, do you understand this part of God's plan of redemption for mankind? The definition of "fruitfruits" is this: Firstfruits are the first gathered fruits of a harvest. Pentecost (or the Feast of Firstfruits) represents the spring harvest, which in the spiritual realm, as well as in the natural, is the smallest harvest.

God is calling out His firstfruits, which He will gather to Himself in the end time, a small group who has matured while living on earth, growing in grace and knowledge, empowered by His Holy Spirit, walking in obedience to God's commandments as Jesus did, and conforming into His very image.

God uses an agricultural term to help us understand a spiritual truth. Have you ever noticed on a tomato plant that one tomato on the vine ripens before the others? One becomes red, while the others are still green. One tomato becomes fully mature, ready to pick, before the others, yet all of the tomatoes are on the same vine. This is what is happening in the spiritual realm of the church.

We all develop at different rates. This is brought out in the parable of the sower (Matt. 13). How the seed (the Word of God) is received is based on the condition of the ground (the heart). It is God, the Father, who prepares the heart. Jesus said in John 6:44: "No man can come to me except the Father which hath sent me draw him." Based upon the condition of the heart, growth rate varies, bringing forth "some an hundredfold, some sixty, some thirty" (Matt. 13:23). Could it be that those believers who produced and received a hundredfold blessing are the firstfruits, the Bride of Christ, worthy to rule and reign with Christ? Notice Jesus's response to his disciples in Matthew 19:28-29 when asked the question, "We have forsaken all [we have given up everything this world has to offer] and have followed you; what shall we have therefore [what is our reward]?"

> And Jesus said unto them, Verily I say unto you, that you
> which have followed me, in the regeneration [the kingdom

of God] when the Son of man shall sit in the throne of his glory, you also shall sit upon twelve thrones, judging the twelve tribes of Israel. And every one that hath forsaken [given up] houses, or brethren, or sisters, or father, or mother, or wife, or children, or lands, for my name's sake, shall receive an hundredfold, and shall inherit everlasting life [in the kingdom of God].

Wow! Did you notice what Jesus said? Have you forsaken everything for Him? Didn't He forsake everything for us? Have you notice that forsaking everything as He did is a requirement to rule and reign with Him, to be His Bride?

What does it mean to forsake everything for His name's sake? It simply means obey Him, to give up your will for His will. It means to walk in obedience to His Word, which means obey His commandments. Jesus forsook all by keeping His Father's commandments ("not my will, but your will be done"). Everything the Father told Him to do, Jesus did. Do you have the courage to remain celibate until marriage; to not lie, even though the truth may hurt? Do you have the courage to keep the Sabbath Day holy, or to change your diet and eat only clean foods according to Deuteronomy 14, or to keep God's seven feast days (Lev. 23) instead of Christmas and Easter? Do you have the courage to obey God's commandments, even though it may cause problems in relationships, such as with your boss, coworkers, wife, husband, and family?

You might say, "I don't have to do those things. Jesus knows I love Him, and I'm going to heaven because I believe in Jesus as my Savior." My friend, if this is you, Jesus said, "If you love me, keep my commandments" (John 14:15). In John 14:23-24, Jesus says, "If a man love me, he will keep my words; and my Father will love him, and we will come unto him, and make our abode with him. He that loveth me not keepeth not my sayings; and the word which you hear is not mine, but the Father's which sent me."

God, the Father, is calling many to be the firstfruits (the Bride). However, notice Matthew 22:14: Many are called, but few are chosen. This scripture pertains to the Bride. Many are called to be the Bride, but few are chosen to be the Bride. The reason is that many believers in this life will not reach full maturity (the firstfruits) because they are not willing to forsake all, and consequently, they will not be chosen (picked) to be the Bride. Again, we are speaking here of reward and not salvation of the soul.

With this truth of the firstfruits as a background, let's look at a few familiar scriptures. In Romans 8:23, Paul writes this: "And not only they, but ourselves also, which have the firstfruits of the Spirit." Paul understood there was a special group called "firstfruits" and that he was a part of it. He mentions it again in Romans 16:5 when speaking of his beloved friend Epaenetus, "who is the firstfruits of Achaia unto Christ."

In 1 Corinthians 15:22-23, Paul says this: "For as in Adam all die, even so in Christ shall all be made alive. But every man in his own order." Did you catch that? Not every believer will be resurrected at the same time. Notice the order: Christ the firstfruits [Christ is the first of the firstfruits: 1 Cor. 15:20]; afterward, they who are Christ's (those who have forsaken all) at His coming (for his Bride). Remember that it is the firstfruits whom the Father called and chose to belong to Christ. It is the firstfruits, the Bride, who will be in the first resurrection when Christ comes for His Bride. Revelation 20:6 says:

> Blessed and holy is he that hath part in the first resurrection: on such the second death hath no power, but they shall be priests [ministers, leaders] of God and of Christ, and shall reign with him a thousand years.

Now I want you to notice what Jesus said about the Father's will:

> And this is the Father's will which hath sent me, that of all which he hath given me [the firstfruits] I should lose nothing, but should raise it [the firstfruits] up again at the last day [in the end times at the first resurrection]. And this is the will of him that sent me, that every one which seeth the Son, and believeth on him, may have everlasting life: and I will raise him up at the last day (John 6:39-40).

Jesus makes it clear that of all that the Father gives Him, He will lose none. This pertains to the firstfruits only. Now look at the second sentence: Jesus emphatically states that it is the will of the Father that all believers have the potential to become firstfruits (may have eternal life). But the Father knows that most will not commit to the sanctified way of life. Jesus said it best in Matt. 7:14:

> Strait is the gate and narrow is the way, which leadeth unto life [*zoe* life—Strong's #2222], and few there be that find it.

The "life" Jesus is talking about is God life, the life that will be reserved for the Bride, a life that goes beyond just living forever, a life called eternal life. Jesus speaks of two types of life: eternal life and everlasting life. Notice John 3:14-16. The setting of these words is where Jesus is talking to Nicodemus, a Pharisee, about the kingdom of God:

> And as Moses lifted up the serpent in the wilderness, even so must the Son of man [Jesus] be lifted up: that whosoever believeth in him should not perish, but have eternal life. For God so loved the world that he gave his only begotten Son, that whosoever believeth in him should not perish, but have everlasting life.

Eternal life stresses quality of life (God life), where everlasting life stresses duration (forever). Those in the world who believe in Jesus as their Redeemer (believe in the blood) receive everlasting life. However, not all believers receive eternal life, because not all will be willing to travel the straight and narrow road.

Jesus, on the night leading up to His Crucifixion, while praying to His Father, makes a powerful statement about the truth of eternal life that has escaped the Christian world. Notice what he says in John 17:3:

> And this is life eternal, that they might know you [Father] the only true God, and Jesus Christ whom you have sent.

The word *know* here is Strong's word #1097, which "indicates a relation between the person 'knowing' and the object known; in this respect, what is 'known' is of value or importance to the one who knows, and hence the establishment of the relationship."

Do you know God? Do you have a relationship with Him? Do you know what He wants you to do? Do you know how He wants you to live to have eternal life?

The story of the rich young man in Matthew 19:16-22 bears out this truth about eternal life. To paraphrase the story, the rich young man comes to Jesus, asking, "What good thing shall I do, that I may have eternal life [that I may go deeper in my relationship with God]?" Jesus answers him by saying, "If you want to go deeper in your walk with God, keep His commandments" [keep in covenant relationship]." Please keep in mind the young man was Jewish and seeking a closer relationship with God, not seeking salvation.

The young man responds to Jesus's answer by inquiring which commandments. After hearing Jesus's list of commandments of how to love your neighbor, the young man states, "All these things have I kept from my youth up until now: what else do I lack?" The young man knew there was more to going deeper with God than loving your neighbor; that is why he asked, "What else do I lack?"

Then Jesus gives him the answer that is hard for believers today to accept: "If you want to be perfect [If you want to be spiritually mature, to go deeper in your relationship with God], sell all that you have [give up your life] and follow me [live like I live, walking in obedience to the Father, loving God with your whole heart, soul, mind, and strength]" (Mark 12:30). And then Jesus adds, "If you will do these things, you shall have treasure in heaven" (you will receive the highest reward of eternal life, being chosen the Bride of Christ).

This eternal life is what Paul was referring to in 1 Corinthians 2:9:

Eye has not seen, nor ear heard, neither have entered into the heart of man, the things which God has prepared for them that love him.

Again, eternal life is connected with firstfruits. James understood firstfruits. He put it this way: "Of his [the Father's] own will begat he us with the word of truth, that we should be a kind of firstfruits of his [creation]" (James 1:18).

Perhaps, for some, I have not made a strong case concerning this special group called firstfruits. Or, at the least, I have not fully convinced you that the firstfruits is the Bride. If that is you, I have a few more scriptures, which I believe will cast out all doubt. It is found in Revelation 14:1-4:

And I looked, and, lo, a Lamb stood on the mount Sion [heavenly Jerusalem], and with him an hundred forty and four thousand, having his Father's name written in their foreheads.

And I heard a voice from heaven, as the voice of many waters, and as the voice of a great thunder: and I heard the voice of harpers harping with their harps:

And they [the hundred and forty-four thousand] sung as it were a new song before the throne, and before the four beasts, and the elders: and no man could learn that song but the hundred and forty and four thousand, which were redeemed from the earth.

These are they which were not defiled with women; for they are virgins. These are they which follow the Lamb whither-soever he goeth. These were redeemed from among men, being the firstfruits unto God and to the Lamb.

Let's break down each verse and draw out nuggets of profound truth, letting the Bible interpret the Bible.

Verse 1 sets the scene, which is Mount Zion, or heavenly Jerusalem (see Heb. 12:22). Here, John sees the Lamb, Jesus Christ, with a group of a hundred and forty-four thousand, which have the Father's name written in their foreheads. Who is this group? In Revelation 3:7-12, Jesus speaks of a special group (the Philadelphia church) who has a little strength (has little power), kept His Word (obeyed His commandments), and has not denied His name (has a deep abiding love for Him).

To this group, He says, "I will write upon him the name of my God." These hundred and forty-four thousand represent this special group (see chapter 10 about the Philadelphia church).

It is important to note that this group has the "Father's name written in their forehead," meaning that this group is special unto the Father because He has personally called and chosen them; they have a special relationship with Him.

In verse 2, we see the scene shift to the very throne of God. Here, the voice of many waters is heard, which is Jesus (see Rev. 1:15), and the voice of thunder is heard, which is God, the Father (see Ps. 77:18), and the "harpers harping with their harps," which are the four beasts and the twenty-four elders (see Rev. 5:8).

Next, in verse 3, we see this special group of a hundred and forty-four thousand singing a new song before the throne of God, where Jesus and God, the Father, and the four beasts with the twenty-four elders are. It was a song that only pertained to them (the hundred and forty-four thousand). No other man could learn that song because it was reserved for this special group.

Why do you think the song was reserved only for them? The answer is given in the last part of verse 3—because they were the first redeemed (the firstfruits) from the earth. (It must be understood that the definition of the redeemed is "those who have been blood washed, born again, and have received their redeemed bodies through a resurrection.")

Could this special group (the firstfruits) be also the Bride? Verse 4 gives the answer. It says, "These are they which were not defiled with women; for they are virgins." The phrase "defiled with women" is a reference to spiritual harlotry and idolatry. Jesus makes mention of this in the book of Revelation, where He hits hard the fact that deceiving spirits come into the church and seduce His people in committing spiritual fornication, going after false gods through false doctrines, "to teach and to seduce my servants to commit fornication, and to eat things sacrificed unto idols" (Rev. 2:20). Notice it says that these hundred and forty-four thousand are virgins. Do you remember the five wise virgins, those who heard the Word of God and lived by it? It was accounted unto them righteousness, enabling them to enter into the bridal chamber.

Now notice the remainder of verse 4. It says, "These are they which follow the Lamb [Christ] whither-soever he goeth." In other words, the Bride has the distinction of always being in the presence of God. This is not true for all of mankind (more on this later). And if there is any doubt who the hundred and forty-four thousand are, the last sentence makes it very clear. These are they who "were redeemed from among men, being the firstfruits unto God and to the Lamb." These hundred and forty-four thousand firstfruits represent the Bride of Christ, being the first redeemed, having their glorified bodies.

As an aside, many believe that the hundred and forty-four thousand mentioned in Revelation 7 is the same group mentioned in Revelation 14. With the above detailed explanation, it is clear that these are two distinct groups. In Revelation 7, the hundred and forty-four thousand are clearly defined as twelve thousand from each of the twelve tribes of Israel listed. These are the children of Israel who have been sealed with the Spirit of God for protection during the Great Tribulation on earth. These will be used as the core group of human beings of the nation Israel during the thousand-year reign of Jesus Christ on earth. The Bride is not restricted to just the twelve tribes of Israel.

It can be noted that God uses the number twelve (or any multiple of twelve) to represent divine government or divine authority, such as the twelve apostles, the twelve tribes of Israel, the twenty-four elders, and the hundred and forty-four thousand firstfruits. With this principle in mind, could it be that the hundred and forty-four thousand is the actual and true number of believers God has in mind who will qualify to make up the Bride of Christ?

Now remember: God is not speaking about the number of people who will be saved. That number is huge. Just look at how many will be saved, which will come out of the Great Tribulation:

> A great multitude which no man could number of all nations, and kindreds, and people (Rev. 7:9).

Yes, a hundred and forty-four thousand is a small number when compared to the number of human beings who have ever lived. But doesn't Jesus call this elite group "little flock" when he says in Luke 12:32, "Fear not little flock; for it is your Father's good pleasure to give you the kingdom." Doesn't Jesus say that "many are called [to be the Bride], but few are chosen [to be the Bride]" (Matt. 22:14)?

But take heart, my friend. There is good news in all of this. Because Jesus tells us that in this last generation, just prior to His return for His Bride, that many will be called to be first (the firstfruits: the Bride). See Matthew 19:30, Matthew 20:16, and Luke 13:30.

Will you answer the call?

LOVE, LOYALTY, AND ALLEGIANCE

One of the main keys to understanding who and what is the Bride of Christ is to understand the three primary attributes of Jesus Christ, attributes that define the response of those called and chosen to be the Bride. These three attributes are love, loyalty, and allegiance.

These three words are interesting in this respect: They all demand action to support their meaning. For example, how can you understand love without seeing it in action? The Bible tells us that God is love (1 John 4:8) and He manifests that love toward us by the giving of His Son (1 John 4:9 and John 3:16). We also see that "Godly love" manifested in Ephesians 5:25, where it says that Christ "loved the church and gave himself for it." How does the Bride manifest its love for Jesus? Very simply, Jesus gives the answer: "If you love me, keep my commandments." The Bride shows its love for God, the Father, and Christ, the Son, by walking in obedience. Love is not a feeling. It must be demonstrated. It is an action. It is a heart thing.

The same principle applies to loyalty and allegiance. Though these words are similar in meaning, they are more amply understood by how they manifest in the life and character of Jesus Christ.

Loyalty is defined as faithfulness or devotion to a person or group. Properly understood, it is an interpersonal term, meaning it relates or occurs among people. Jesus personifies loyalty. All through the Gospel accounts, we see Jesus's loyalty (faithfulness and devotion) to His Father by yielding up His will to do His Father's will (John 4:34).

Jesus was loyal to His Father by speaking the message the Father gave Him (John 8:28-29; John 12:49-50). My friend, I urge you to read the Gospel accounts and highlight all the scriptures where Jesus demonstrated His loyalty, His deep devotion to His heavenly Father, desiring to glorify God the Father by His life. The number of Bible passages where Jesus showed his loyalty to His Father will amaze you.

Added to this, Jesus demonstrates His deep abiding loyalty to those who believe in Him, to those who desire to walk as He walked. We have it in writing in Hebrews 13:5, where He tells us, "I will never leave you nor forsake you." Loyalty is a Godly trait. We see all through the Bible where God was faithful and loyal to His people, fulfilling His promises, regardless of their sin.

God expects nothing less from His Bride. Jesus will marry a Bride who has demonstrated in his or her lifetime true devotion and loyalty to Him and to the Father, as well as a love for the brethren. Remember that loyalty has to be demonstrated, lived out in your life to be real. How does the Bride demonstrate loyalty? By walking in obedience to the Word of God (no matter the cost), yielding up your will to the Father's will, just like Jesus did—that's how. We can see this loyalty played out in the book of Revelation, as the apostle John writes about the Bride (those who will be ruling and reigning), who paid a supreme price:

> And I saw thrones, and they sat upon them, and judgment was given unto them: and I saw the souls of them that were beheaded for the witness of Jesus and for the Word of God, and which had not worshipped the beast, neither his image, neither had received his mark upon their foreheads, or in their hands; and they lived and reigned with Christ a thousand years (Rev. 20:4).

A term closely associated with the word *loyalty* is allegiance. Where loyalty expresses devotion toward other people, allegiance is properly used when conveying loyalty to a sovereign government. *Allegiance* can be defined as a duty or act of loyalty owed by citizens to their sovereign government. For example, we demonstrate our allegiance to the United States of America each time we cite the Pledge of Allegiance or stand during the playing of our National Anthem.

In our case as Christians, this term, *allegiance*, should help us to understand our right and proper relationship with the kingdom (or government) of God. When we accept Jesus Christ as our Lord and Savior, we become born again, born into the kingdom (or the family of God), becoming citizens of the kingdom, whereby we owe our allegiance as a result of our birth. In other words, if you were born in America and are a born-again believer, you hold dual citizenships.

It is unfortunate that the knowledge of the kingdom of God has been lost upon the hearts and minds of the believer. Jesus came with a message from the Father: a good news message of the kingdom of God. He came to usher in the kingdom (or government) of God here on earth. By coming to earth, Jesus Christ reconnected us to the Father and to His glorious kingdom by the power of the Holy Spirit.

Jesus tells the believer that "it is the Father's good pleasure to give you [born-again sons and daughters] the Kingdom" (Luke 12:32).

The apostle Paul understood this reconnection to the kingdom when he said, "Now then we are Ambassadors for Christ" (2 Cor. 5:20). Ambassadors are fully authorized to represent their government, reflecting the views and policies of the head of government. As born-again, blood-bought believers in Jesus Christ, we have been called to be ambassadors to represent the kingdom of God here on earth. Does your life reflect the views and policies of your heavenly Father? Do you back up and support the laws of the kingdom by your lifestyle and behavior? This is what it means to be in allegiance with the kingdom (or government) of God.

Jesus demonstrated His allegiance to the kingdom by announcing its arrival, living in harmony with its laws, speaking for and representing the views of His Father, and supporting it to the fullest, climaxed by His death. His Bride should do no less.

THE PHILADELPHIANS

We saw in chapter 3 that God has reserved unto Himself a special group, called His jewels. In Malachi 3:17, we read:

> And they shall be mine, saith the Lord of host, in that day when I make up my jewels; and I will spare them, as a man spareth his own son that serveth [loves and worships] him.

This prophetic verse points to the future. Here we see that "in that day" (at the time of Jesus's return), God will protect this special group (His jewels, the Bride).

We see this special group mentioned in the book of Revelation, only this time, it is veiled behind the name of the Philadelphia church (Philadelphians). Notice Revelation 3:10:

> Because you [Philadelphians] have kept the word of my patience, I also will keep you from the hour of temptation [a time of great adversity, affliction, or hardship], which shall come upon all the world, to try them [to put them to the test] that dwell upon the earth.

Of the seven churches described in Revelation 2 and 3 (these churches represent seven different conditions of the end-time church), only the Philadelphians are special unto God to merit His protection from the "hour of temptation." What was special about this group, the Philadelphians, that God will spare them, protect them from the Great Tribulation that will come upon all the earth?

Jesus reveals special characteristics of the Philadelphians that are not included in the messages to the other six churches.

In verse 8, He says the following:

- You have a little strength (you are weak in spiritual power).
- You have kept my word (you have been obedient).
- You have not denied my name (you have been loyal and faithful to me).

In verse 10, Jesus says of this special group: "Because you have kept the word of my patience." "The word of my [God's] patience" can be better understood as the "patience of the saints," as defined in Revelation 14:12:

> Here is the patience of the saints: here are they that keep
> the commandments of God, and the faith of Jesus.

Letting the Word interpret the Word, verse 10 reads as follows:

"Because you have patiently waited on the promises of my word to be fulfilled by keeping the commandments of God and the faith of Jesus, I also will keep you from the time of Great Tribulation."

Notice the similarities between the jewels in Malachi 3:16-17 with Malachi 4:4 and the Philadelphians in Revelation 3:8, 10:

Malachi 3:16-17; 4:4	Revelation 3:8, 10
They that feared the Lord.	You have kept my word.
They that thought upon his name	You have not denied my name.
I will spare them.	I will keep them.

Remember the law of Moses: "Because you have the commandments of God and the faith of Jesus."

I believe without a doubt these passages in Revelation refer to a very select and special group, known as the Bride of Christ.

To support my conclusion that the church of Philadelphia (the Philadelphians) represents the Bride, let's consider the nuggets revealed in verses 11 and 12. Remember that the role of the Bride is to be kings and priests in the kingdom of God, ruling and reigning with Christ forever.

In verse 11, Jesus is warning His Bride:

> Behold I come quickly: Hold fast that which you have [hold fast to the truth] so that no man take your crown [so that no man, woman, or devil deceive you that you should lose your reward of kingship].

As a side note to this verse, we need to go back to verses 7 and 8 to see something that God says about the nature of those called to be the Bride. Verses 7 and 8 refer to "no man"; the Greek word translated *man* in English is Strong's #3762, which means "none, nobody, or nothing" (not "man," which is Strong's #444).

In other words, Jesus is making a powerful point in these two verses that says, "no body, not even Satan himself," can prevent what He wants to accomplish through His Bride on earth, even though those whom He is calling to be His Bride may be lacking in spiritual power ["you have a little strength"].

In verse 12, Jesus makes some astonishing statements that pertain to the Bride and are reinforced in other passages of Revelation, as shown in brackets below:

> To him who overcometh [to him who overcomes as I [Jesus] have overcome, Rev. 3:21], will I make a pillar in the temple of my God [will I grant to sit with me in my

throne, Rev. 3:21] and he shall go no more out [he shall not be separated from Christ but shall follow the Lamb wherever He goes, Rev. 14:4] and I will write upon him the name of my God [being part of the hundred and forty-four thousand, having His Father's name written in their foreheads, Rev. 14:1] and the name of the city of my God, which is new Jerusalem [which indicates and identifies the Bride, the Lamb's wife, Rev. 21:9] and I will write upon him my new name [which no man knows but Christ Himself, Rev. 19:12].

When put together, these nuggets of truth reveal the awesome mystery of the Bride of Christ.

As a sidebar to verse 12 of Revelation 3, I want to draw your attention to something very profound that is lost upon most who study Revelation. In verse 12, Jesus mentions "him that overcometh," and then He lists the rewards given to those who overcome (*overcome* means "get the victory"; see Strong's #3528).

Jesus closes out each message to the seven churches with this declaration to the "overcomer." What is profound about this description of overcomer is that it describes who and what the Bride is: an overcomer, one who gets the victory over Satan, just as Jesus did at the cross. Just as it was Jesus's victory over the devil that qualified him to "sit down with [His] Father in his throne" (Rev. 3:21), so it will be for the Bride who gets the victory over Satan, qualifying to rule and reign with Christ.

Getting victory is a vital truth that must be understood. In chapter 2, it was brought out that man was created to have dominion (rulership and authority) over all the earth, and that dominion included having authority over Satan, the devil, and his kingdom, which Jesus Christ won for mankind at the cross. Satan is a defeated foe, but we have to take our authority to get the victory over him.

By ending each message to the churches with the declaration to the overcomer, Jesus is encouraging the body of Christ by saying this:

No matter what condition you may be in: lost your first love (Rev. 2:4), suffered persecution (Rev. 2:10), given to deception (Rev. 2:14-15), allowed false doctrine and witchcraft to seduce you (Rev. 2-20), produced dead works (Rev. 3:1), have little strength (Rev. 3:8), become lukewarm (Rev. 3:16), if you hang tough, continue to wage war against the enemy who wants to destroy you and your destiny, and get the victory over him in your life, the highest reward is reserved for you: to become the Bride.

The Bride is one who is a warrior for Christ. The Bride is one who understands spirit world realities, who understands where the fight is, knowing it is not "against flesh and blood [meaning, the fight is not against ourselves or other people] but against principalities, against powers, against the rulers of darkness of this world, against spiritual wickedness in high places" (Eph. 6:12). The Bride is one who has been equipped by the Holy Spirit with the mighty weapons of warfare and uses them by faith against the enemy to get the victory.

Notice the list of rewards given to "him who overcometh"—the Bride:

1. shall eat of the tree of life (Rev. 2:7)
2. shall not be hurt of the second death (Rev. 2:11)
3. will eat of the hidden manna; will receive a white-stone with a new name which no man knows (Rev. 2:17)
4. will be given power over the nations and shall rule them with a rod of iron (Rev. 2:26-27)
5. will be clothed in white raiment and whose name will not be blotted out of the Book of Life (Rev. 3:5)
6. will be a pillar in the temple of God; will forever be in the presence of God; will have written upon him the name of God, the name of new Jerusalem, and the new name of Jesus Christ (Rev. 3:12)
7. will be granted the privilege to sit with Jesus Christ in His throne (to rule and reign with Him) (Rev. 3:21)

Are you ready for another nugget of truth? Are you ready to peel back more understanding from the Word of God, revealing more of the mystery of the Bride? Jesus identifies Himself to the Philadelphians as "he that has [or holds] the key of David." Jesus understood the key of David. Do we understand what this key of David is all about? Could it be that those who represent Philadelphians today understand the key of David?

The Bible makes it very clear that David was very special to God. Of David's character, God says in Acts 13:22, "I have found David the son of Jesse, a man after mine own heart, which shall fulfill all my will." David's name in Hebrew means "beloved, an intimate," an endearing name God uses when He talks about His Bride in Song of Solomon 6:3: "I am my beloved's, and my beloved is mine:" Could it be that David was like Jesus Christ?

What many do not realize is that Jesus Christ reveals Himself as a mighty warrior and a passionate worshipper. Many will be surprised to learn that Jesus was the God of the Old Testament (see 1 Cor. 10:1-4). In Exodus 15:3, after God (who later became Jesus) destroyed the Egyptian army, the nation Israel sang: "The LORD is a man of war [warrior]: the LORD is his name." In Joshua 5:13-15, we see another example of the one who became Jesus who appeared as a man of war before Joshua. Please read this account because it powerfully shows the warrior nature of God; it reveals that the One who became Jesus, our Savior, was the Commander of the Army of God in heaven.

As a sidebar, I urge the reader to research the subject "Theophanies in the Old Testament," where theophanies are examples of the preincarnate Christ, when God took on human form and appeared before humans.

Worship is the heart of Jesus. While on earth, Jesus worshipped His Father by His profound reverence, love, and veneration for Him, demonstrated by His obedience. Everything the Father told Him to say and do, Jesus obeyed. (Please remember this: Obedience is the greatest form of worship.) Jesus understood the principle "To obey is better than sacrifice" (1 Sam. 15:22). Not only was Jesus a worshipper of the Father, but He was passionate about it. Notice the account in John 2:13-16 and in Matthew 21:12-13, where Jesus "went into the temple of God, and cast out all them that sold and bought in the temple, and over threw the tables of the moneychangers, and the seats of them that sold doves and said unto them, 'Take these things hence; make not my Father's house an house of merchandise.'"

Just as Jesus was and is a mighty warrior and a passionate worshipper, so too was David. These two quality character traits, alone, emphasize why David was characterized as "a man after [God's] heart."

We read of the mighty warrior exploits of David in battle, from slaying Goliath to defeating the Philistines and other enemy nations. David had to defeat a physical enemy who wanted to destroy him, while we today have to defeat a spiritual enemy who wants to destroy us.

We have David's many psalms today, which reveal his heart and devotion for God and describe how he worshipped with all of his being. Notice, for example, Psalm 9:1-2: "I will praise you, O LORD, with my whole heart; I will show forth all your marvelous works. I will be glad and rejoice in you: I will sing praise to your name, O you most High." In Psalm 119:97, David says, "O how love I thy law [Torah]! It is my meditation all the day." David was so passionate about worshipping Elohim, the God of the Universe, that he instituted the Tabernacle of David, where he set up a tent to worship God in songs and praise twenty-four hours a day. Also, within the Tabernacle of David was housed the Ark of the Covenant, where the very presence of God resided until the Ark was moved into the Holy of Holies within the new temple built by Solomon.

David was faithful to God's government by demonstrating his allegiance to his earthly king, King Saul, who represented the anointing (and government) of God on earth, even though Saul sought to kill him (see 1 Sam. 24:6). David loved God, and he showed his love by his obedience to God's Word, keeping His statutes and commandments (1 Kings 11:33).

David loved God's law and wrote about his devotion to it in Psalm 119. He understood and obeyed the requirement to be king, and this edict holds true today for the Bride, who is in preparation to be king. Notice these powerful verses in Deuteronomy 17:18-19:

And it shall be, when he sitteth upon the throne of his kingdom, that he shall write him a copy of this law [the Torah] in a book out of that which is before the priests the Levites: and it shall be with him, and he shall read therein all the days of his life: that he may learn to fear the LORD his God, to keep all the words of this law and these statutes, to do them.

Now notice what he writes in Psalm 19:7-11:

The law of the LORD is perfect, converting the soul: the testimony of the LORD is sure, making wise the simple. The statutes of the LORD are right, rejoicing the heart: the commandment of the LORD is pure, enlightening the eyes. The fear of the LORD is clean, enduring for ever: the judgments of the LORD are true and righteous altogether. More to be desired are they than gold, yea, than much fine gold: sweeter also than honey and the honeycomb. Moreover by them is your servant warned: and in keeping of them there is great reward.

Did you catch what David wrote at the end of these verses?

And in keeping of them [God's statutes and commandments] there is great reward.

David understood the connection between living a life of obedience and receiving a great reward. Yet he was not motivated for selfish gain. His outward actions of loyalty, faithfulness, and allegiance were based upon an inner heart of love and devotion toward God. That is why God could say of David that he was "a man after mine own heart" (Acts 13:22). This is the kind of heart Jesus is looking for in the one He marries.

David will be rewarded in the kingdom of God by becoming a part of the Bride of Christ. He has been honored to be king over all the nation of Israel forever, serving directly under Jesus Christ (Ezek. 37:24).

David's character typifies the characteristics of the Bride of Christ:

- a man after God's own heart
- a man greatly beloved by God
- a man who was a mighty warrior for God
- a man who was a worshipper of God
- a man who was faithful and loyal to the government (kingdom) of God
- a man who loved God's law and walked in obedience to the statutes and commandments of God

What is the key of David? Could David be the key that unlocks the mystery of the Bride of Christ? Could the key of David be this: that David was a type of the Bride? I believe the evidence is irrefutable and supports that belief.

The church of Philadelphia represents a body of believers whom God is calling out today to prepare to be the Bride, to prepare to rule and reign with Jesus Christ forever.

The Philadelphian is one who understands that salvation is by faith in the blood of Jesus, and reward is handed out to believers by how they live while on the earth, getting the victory over Satan and his kingdom.

Philadelphians believe in the promise that Jesus will keep them "from the hour of temptation, which shall come upon all the world, to try them that dwell upon the earth."

The Philadelphian understands that the word *Philadelphia* means "brotherly love," and the Philadelphian has a deep love for his brothers and sisters in Christ, desiring for all to reach their destiny, as God has planned and purposed. May God help all of us toward that end.

GOD'S APPOINTED TIMES

During the course of this book, it has been brought out that God desires His people to live by His spiritual laws that He, as Creator, has set in motion for our good. Deuteronomy 6:24 says, "And the LORD commanded us to do all these statutes, to fear the Lord our God, for our good always, that he might preserve us alive."

Keeping God's commandments will "preserve us alive." By keeping God's laws (His commandments), we are walking in righteousness. The next verse (verse 25) makes this very point. Notice what it says:

> And it [God's laws] shall be our righteousness, if we observed to do all these commandments before the LORD our God, as he has commanded us.

It must be remembered that we have our righteousness, based upon how we live by faith, "that the righteousness of the law might be fulfilled [completed] in us, who walk not after the flesh, but after the Spirit" (Rom. 8:4).

It is the righteousness of Jesus Christ that is imputed to us for salvation. (No amount of law keeping can save us.) However, it is how we live on earth that determines our reward. Jesus tells us at the end of the book (Rev. 22:12):

> Behold, I come quickly; and my reward is with me, to give every man according as his work [of obedience] shall be.

As part of God's commandments, He has set in motion appointed times for us to keep for our good. Notice Leviticus 23:1-2:

> And the LORD spoke unto Moses, saying, speak unto the children of Israel, and say unto them, the feasts [appointed times] of the LORD, which you shall proclaim to be holy convocations [commanded assemblies], these are my feasts [my appointed times].

Please notice what God says here. He says "these are my feasts," "the feasts of the LORD." He does not say these feasts are "the Jews' feasts" or "Israel's feasts." Isn't that interesting? Yet it is widely held in Christendom that the feasts as mentioned in Leviticus 23 and elsewhere are strictly Israel's. Very few realize that these feasts, along with the weekly Sabbath and other laws mentioned in the Torah (instruction in righteousness), were and are intended by God to be observed by all of mankind, Jews and Gentiles alike.

I want to share with you some nuggets of truth in God's written word, the Bible, as it concerns these feasts and Sabbaths, scriptures that have been overlooked for centuries but now God is shining the light of truth on them.

Numbers 15:15-16 says:

> One ordinance [law] shall be both for you of the congregation [Israel, God's covenant people], and also for the stranger [Gentiles] that sojourneth with you, an ordinance forever in your generations; as you are, so shall the stranger be, before the Lord. One law [Torah: instruction in righteousness] and one manner [of living]

shall be for you, and for the stranger that sojourneth with you.

I like how the New International Version says it:

The community is to have the same rules for you and for the foreigner residing among you; this is a lasting ordinance for the generations to come. You and the foreigner shall be the same before the LORD: The same laws and regulations will apply both to you and to the foreigner residing among you.

In other words, the Creator God was making it very specific that He had only one law (which includes keeping the feast days), and it was for all mankind to live by.

Keeping the feasts of the Lord are very important to God, so much so that obedience to keeping these feast days will carry over into the millennium, when Christ sets up His kingdom on earth. Notice what the prophet Zechariah says in Zechariah 14:16-18:

And it shall come to pass, that every one that is left of all the [Gentile] nations which came against Jerusalem [this refers to those nations that came through the great tribulation into the time of Christ's reign on earth] shall even go up from year to year to worship the King, the LORD of hosts, and to keep the feast of tabernacles. And it shall be, that whoso will not come up of all [Gentile] families of the earth unto Jerusalem to worship the King, the LORD of hosts, even upon them shall be no rain. And if the family of Egypt go not up, and come not, that have no rain; there shall be the plague, wherewith the LORD will smite the heathen that come not up to keep the feast of tabernacles. This shall be the punishment of Egypt, and the punishment of all nations that come not up to keep the feast of tabernacles.

The book of Isaiah has much to say about the time when Jesus Christ sets up His kingdom on earth. I urge you, the reader, to take the time and study this book. In the last chapter, chapter 66, verse 23, please notice these powerful words of our Creator God:

> And it shall come to pass [in the millennium], that from one new moon to another [this is a reference to God's calendar and His feast days], and from one Sabbath to another, shall all flesh [all mankind] come to worship before me, saith the Lord.

I hope you can see the nuggets of truth in these scriptures. The Christian world believes that God has laws and days for Jews and different laws and days for Christians. That teaching is a lie from the pit of hell. As you have seen, God has one law (Torah) and special days (Sabbaths and feasts) to keep for all mankind, and He desires that we learn of His ways, His days, His feasts.

Now, let's return back to Leviticus 23 and learn some more about God's feasts.

> And the LORD spoke unto Moses, saying, speak unto the children of Israel, and say unto them, concerning the feasts of the LORD, which you shall proclaim to be holy convocations, even these are my feasts (Lev. 23:2-3).

The word *feasts* used here is Strong's #4150, which means "appointed time, a fixed time or season, an appointment." Why did God design these appointed times? Is there a purpose that God had in mind for instituting these days? Most assuredly, yes.

God is a God of purpose. And He has designed His appointed times to keep His people in the true memory and the true worship of the one true God. This was done by having God's people re-enact year after year (in memorial) the seven appointed feast times, revealing the whole story of spiritual regeneration, of how God was reproducing Himself through mankind, bringing about His plans and purposes of restoring the kingdom of God back to earth.

Now, let's go to Leviticus 23:3, and see something profound:

> Six days shall work be done: but the seventh day is the Sabbath of rest, an holy convocation; you shall do no work therein; it is the Sabbath of the Lord in all your dwellings.

Here we find the weekly Sabbath is included with the appointed times (feasts) of God; the seventh day as Sabbath is a holy commanded assembly (holy convocation), a day of rest in which no work is done, a Sabbath of the Lord.

As we go through the seven feasts of God, we will see that each of the feast days is considered a Sabbath, wherein it is designated a day of rest (wherein no work is done) and a day of commanded assembly.

As an aside, it is to be noted that God desires His people to assemble together (commanded assembly) on these Sabbath feast days. The primary purpose for this assembling together is threefold:

1. To rest from the weekly grind of physical labor and enjoy God's creation
2. To form bonds of friendship with fellow believers
3. To focus on the things of God, being reminded of and instructed in the importance of living by God's instructions in righteousness

However, the reality is that it's very difficult to assemble together with people of like minds who understand kingdom living and the importance of covenant relationships because the numbers are few. For this reason, our assembling together may instead be with our family at home, studying God's Word, and enjoying a walk in the park.

The bottom line is this: Keeping the weekly Sabbath and the annual feasts is all about building relationships, first with our heavenly Father and His Son, Jesus Christ, and with others who understand covenant living.

These feasts are filled with rich symbolism and meaning, which come to light through the understanding of this hermeneutic principle: "The New Testament is the Old Testament revealed." We, under the New Testament dispensation, have much more understanding of these feast days than the members of the early church.

We have the privilege of looking back at these days as God revealed them to ancient Israel and seeing through the New Testament the deep, rich, spiritual meaning of these appointed times as they relate to the church today. For the early church, these feast days were "shadows of things to come" (see Col. 2:16-17), but for the church today (for those who have eyes to see and ears to hear), these feast days, or annual Sabbaths, represent the reality, the true plan of salvation for all of mankind, a profound truth that God desires His Bride to embrace.

So let's look at some basic truths as contained in these appointed times (feast days), beginning with a brief breakdown and then a description of God's feasts and holy days (annual Sabbaths).

There are seven annual feasts (appointed times):

1. Passover
2. Feast of Unleavened Bread
3. Pentecost
4. Feast of Trumpets
5. Day of Atonement
6. Feast of Tabernacles
7. Last Great Day

There are seven annual feast days (annual Sabbaths):

1. First Day of Unleavened Bread
2. Seventh Day of Unleavened Bread
3. Day of Pentecost
4. Day of Trumpets
5. Day of Atonement

6. First Day of Tabernacles
7. Last Great Day

Passover

Passover is a commanded assembly but not a holy day because work is allowed in preparation of what immediately follows, which is the seven-day period called the Feast of Unleavened Bread.

Passover is kept at evening time (after sunset), at the beginning of the fourteenth day of the first month, according to God's sacred calendar (see Holy Day calendar in the appendix for dates of feast days). The focus on this day is Jesus Christ, our Passover Lamb. Specifically, this day represents the first part of God's plan of salvation for mankind, where we put our faith in the blood of the Lamb, Jesus Christ, our Redeemer, to become born again.

The Passover ceremony is a simple yet powerful service where believers gather to remember Christ's last night on earth as a human being, with a foot washing (men washing men's feet and women washing women's feet) and the taking of unleavened bread and wine, commemorating the beaten body and shed blood of our Savior. A reading of the scriptures, such as Matthew 26:26-30, John 13:1-17, and John chapters 14 through 17, make this Passover service unforgettable.

Feast of Unleavened Bread

The next part of God's plan of salvation, after we have our sins forgiven and become born again by faith in the blood of the Lamb, Jesus Christ, is to teach us to live a righteous life, to walk in covenant relationship with our Creator God by being obedient to His laws. This is demonstrated by keeping the Feast of Unleavened Bread, which represents getting sin out of your life by removing leavening products (sin) from your "house" (your body) and eating unleavened bread for seven days (picturing living righteously).

The first and seventh day of this feast are holy days (annual Sabbaths), which means you should not go to work on these days but rest, giving honor to your heavenly Father and focusing on the rich meaning of these days. (The apostle Paul kept this feast; see 1 Cor. 5:6-8.)

Pentecost

The next phase of God's plan for mankind, after becoming born again and living righteously (walking in covenant with God by obeying His Word), is the awesome calling to become the firstfruits of God. This event is represented by the Feast of Pentecost.

The name *Pentecost* means "count fifty" and comes from the fact that this day is determined from fifty days from the wave sheaf offering during the Feast of Unleavened Bread. It is always on a Sunday because the wave sheaf offering is always on the Sunday (or first day of the week) during the days of unleavened bread.

However, the more appropriate name of this feast is Feast of Firstfruits (see Ex. 23:16, Ex.34:22), a time which recognizes the firstfruits of the spring (or first) harvest. As was brought out in chapter 6, in this feast, God calls out His Bride, those who have matured in Christ, being led, fed, and guided by the Holy Spirit, to be chosen to be with Him for all eternity. The day is a holy day, being an annual Sabbath, which means a day of rest, honoring our great God. It is a day to focus on God's plan for mankind, especially on the Bride of Christ, whom God, the Father, is preparing to marry Christ.

Feast of Trumpets

This feast has tremendous meaning when fully understood. When God was revealing His appointed times (feast days) to the nation Israel, as outlined in Leviticus 23, He had very little to say about this appointed time. Let's notice what is revealed in verses 24 and 25:

1. The day is to be kept on the first day of the seventh month.
2. It is to be an annual Sabbath, a holy convocation, a day of rest, and an offering is to be given.
3. It is to be a "memorial of blowing of trumpets."

The only understanding ancient Israel had of the blowing of trumpets at the time God revealed this feast day to them was when He announced Himself to the people at Mount Sinai. It was here that God was going to personally intervene in the affairs of men, preceded by the voice of the trumpet. The account is given in Exodus 19. Here are the highlights:

1. God told Moses that He was coming to him in a thick cloud so that "the people may hear when I speak with you and believe you forever" (verse 9).
2. God told Moses to get the people cleaned up, ready to meet Him, for in three days, He was coming "down in the sight of all the people upon Mount Sinai" (verses 10, 11).
3. God told Moses how the people were to approach Mount Sinai, by coming near but not touching, and when they heard the trumpet sounding long, "they shall come up to the mount" (verses 12, 13).
4. On the third day in the morning, God announced His coming with thunder and lightning and a thick cloud upon the mount, where the people heard "the voice of the trumpet exceeding loud; so that all the people that were in the camp trembled" (verse 16).
5. "And when the voice of the trumpet sounded long, and waxed louder and louder, Moses spake, and God answered him by a voice" (verse 19).

This was an amazing event, when Almighty God personally came down to earth and revealed Himself to His people by the voice of the trumpet.

We see this happening again in the end times when Almighty God, Jesus Christ, personally intervenes in the affairs of His people, by announcing His coming for His Bride by "the voice of the trumpet."

God revealed this mystery of Christ coming for His Bride to the apostle Paul, and he wrote about it to the Thessalonians and the Corinthians:

"For this we say unto you by the word of the Lord, that we [who have qualified to be the Bride] which are alive and remain unto the coming of the Lord shall not prevent [proceed] them which are asleep [those who have died]. For the Lord himself shall descend from heaven with a shout [a cry of excitement], with the voice of the archangel, and with the trump [voice] of God: and the dead in Christ shall rise first: Then we which are alive and remain shall be caught up together with them in the clouds, to meet the Lord in the air: and so shall we ever be with the Lord" (1 Thess. 4:15-17).

"Behold I show you a mystery; We shall not all sleep, but we shall all be changed, in a moment, in the twinkling of an eye, at the last [utmost, greatest] trump: for the trumpet shall sound, and the dead shall be raised incorruptible, and we shall be changed" (1 Cor. 15:52).

In the book of Revelation, we read about the "the seven angels which had the seven trumpets prepared themselves to sound" (Rev. 8:6). In Revelation 11:15, we see where the seventh angel sounds the trumpet, declaring "the kingdoms of this world are become the kingdoms of our Lord, and of his Christ; and he shall reign for ever and ever." This sounding of the seventh trumpet pictures the event in Revelation 19:14-15, where Jesus Christ personally intervenes in human affairs, coming with His Bride to rule and reign on earth.

Whereas Pentecost pictures the calling of the first fruits, the Feast of Trumpets pictures two significant, world-changing events, which are heralded by the blowing of trumpets:

1. Christ coming for His Bride, his firstfruits
2. Christ returning with His Bride to rule and reign with him on earth

This Day of Trumpets is a high day or Sabbath, which means it is a day of rest and a commanded assembly. It is a day of celebration. Observe this day with gladness. Make it special with your family, if possible. Focus on these two awesome events, which will be announced by the blowing of trumpets: 1) when Christ comes to take His prepared Bride to heaven for the marriage ceremony, and 2) when Christ returns to earth with His

Bride to rule and reign for a thousand years. It is a day to richly praise and worship our great God.

Day of Atonement

This day has tremendous meaning. It depicts the time after Christ returns with His Bride (pictured by the Feast of Trumpets), when He sets up His kingdom, and human beings on earth become one with their Maker ("at-One-ment" with their God). This can only happen when Satan is dealt with properly. The full meaning of this feast is understood by what the High Priest does on this day (see Lev. 16). He takes two goats for an atonement: one to be offered as a blood sacrifice (representing Jesus Christ) making an atonement for sin, and the other to be sent into the wilderness (the azazel goat, representing Satan). Please notice Leviticus 16:21. Here is the meaning of the symbolism portrayed in this verse, which pictures a time yet to come:

> Our High Priest, Jesus Christ, will lay both his hands on the head of Satan, the devil, and confess over him all the iniquities, transgressions, and sins of mankind upon the head of this spirit being who is responsible for sin. Then Satan will be bound in chains by an angel and cast into the bottomless pit, where he will be shut up and sealed for a thousand years [see Rev. 20:1-3].

Many believers need to get a revelation that all sin is Satan inspired. This feast pictures the reality that Satan will be held accountable for his diabolical deeds and that the sins of mankind will be totally atoned for.

The Day of Atonement is a day of fasting (afflicting your soul), where we become one with our Creator by being led by our spirit and not by our flesh. It is a Sabbath, which means a day of rest. It is a day to focus on the fact that the author of sin, Satan, the devil, will be bound in chains in the bottomless pit for a thousand years, enabling mankind for the first time to live without being under the sway of Satan himself. Halleluiah! Praise God.

Feast of Tabernacles

To summarize so far, this is the plan of salvation for mankind that God reveals in His feasts (appointed times):

The first thing that has to happen is for you to become born again by faith in the blood of the Lamb (Passover). Next, you must live righteously, getting the leaven out (Feast of Unleavened Bread). Next, God is calling His firstfruits to become the Bride (Pentecost). Afterwards, Christ is coming for His Bride, who will be redeemed from the earth before the Great Tribulation, marry Christ in heaven, then return to earth to rule and reign with him during the millennium (Feast of Trumpets), then mankind, during the millennium, is going to live for the first time without Satan's deception, becoming "at-one-ment" with our Creator (Day of Atonement).

What is to follow is nothing short of amazing: the Feast of Tabernacles. This feast pictures the time on earth when God, through Jesus Christ, will come and tabernacle (dwell) with mankind. Another name for this feast is the Feast of Ingathering (see Ex. 23:16, Ex. 34:22) where many will come into the family of God during this thousand-year period, for the knowledge of God will be spread upon the whole earth. It will be unlike any revival we have ever seen.

The Feast of Tabernacles is celebrated over a seven-day period, where the first day is a Sabbath (rest day) and a time to rejoice (Lev. 23:33-35; Deut. 16:13-15).

What a plan God has for us. But wait. It's not over. There is one more feast (appointed time) that God has purposed. It is on the eighth day, or the day following the seven-day period of the Feast of Tabernacles (Lev. 23:36, 39). It is a high day or solemn assembly day, which means it is an annual Sabbath of rest.

Its name is "the Last Great Day," which comes from John 7:37. This day is special unto God. It is a day where Jesus cried, "If any man thirst, let him come unto me and drink. He that believeth on me, as the scripture hath said, out of his belly shall flow rivers of living water." Since it is on the eighth day, it pictures a time of new beginnings, which follows the time of the millennium.

This time corresponds with the period of the White Throne Judgment spoken of in Revelation 20:11-15. Could this be the time when all those human beings who have ever lived but who have never heard the name of Jesus Christ are given a new beginning? Is that why this day is called great? Are these the ones Jesus makes His passionate plea to when He says, "If any man thirst, let him come unto me and drink"? What a way to finish out His plan of salvation for mankind.

Are you beginning to see the rich meaning of these awesome feast days and how important it is for believers to keep them? Those called to be the Bride of Christ in these last days will be moved by the Holy Spirit of God to embrace these days and observe them, just as Jesus kept them when He walked this earth. (See chapter 12 for more information on God's Holy Days and also see the appendix for dates of God's feast days.)

WHERE DO I GO FROM HERE?

If you have read the previous eleven chapters and are moved to take action on what you have learned, you may be asking the question: "Where do I go from here?"

Before answering the question, it is vital to review some very key points.

You must have a revelation that the first and great commandment in the law is that "You shall love the Lord your God with all your heart, with all your soul, and with all your mind (Matt. 22:37-38). In other words, you must have a revelation that obedience to the laws of God (His Torah) is an outward expression of an inward heart of deep gratitude of the Father's love for you by the giving of His Son to pay the ransom price for your sins.

You must have a revelation that obedience to God's law (His instruction in righteousness) is not bondage. It brings freedom. "The truth [Torah] shall make you free" (John 8:32). It is living a life of sin that brings bondage because "sin is the transgression of the law" (1 John 3:4).

You must realize that our obedience is to God's written law and not to the oral law and traditions that the Jews kept (and even keep to this day). It was the oral law and traditions that the Pharisees taught and held in supremacy over God's written Torah. This is what Jesus came against when

He criticized the religious leaders of His day, when He said, "In vain do they worship me, teaching for doctrines the commandments of men [the oral law]. For laying aside the commandment of God [the written law, the Torah], you hold the tradition of men [the oral law] as the washing of pots and cups: and many other such like things you do … full well you reject the commandment of God [the written Torah], that you may keep your own tradition" (Mark 7:7-9).

You must realize that the laws and commandments of God are spiritual and holy, based on love, and that by walking in obedience to these laws, you are being conformed into the very "image and likeness" of God, having the very law of God "written on your heart" (Jer. 31:31-33).

You must understand that your relationship with your heavenly Father is not based on obedience (that is, on what you do) but only on your active faith in your Savior ("for by grace are you saved through faith"). It is your faith in the blood that saves you, because it is your faith in the redemptive work of Jesus Christ (His death, burial, and resurrection) that makes you a child of God. God loves you because you are His child. Therefore, His love for you is not predicated on your obedience. It is based on who you are: His child. Thank God.

However, your Father desires you to obey Him, His Word, His instructions in righteousness (Torah), so that you can become one like Him, a chip off the ol' block. It is through living by His instruction in righteousness that you show your faith and become molded and shaped into the very image of God.

He is not coming to receive an already established, human-designed political system, such as a democracy. God's Word tells us that when Jesus comes, He shall "set up a kingdom which shall never be destroyed and it shall break in pieces and consume [terminate] all [other] kingdoms" (Dan. 2:44). Jesus is coming to establish on earth a theocratic form of government, headed up by Himself (King Jesus), who will delegate His power and authority to a special people called His Bride, who will rule and reign with Him for a thousand years and beyond.

Jesus knows He can trust His Bride with world-ruling power and authority because those who make up the Bride will have proven themselves to be worthy ("has made herself ready," Rev. 21:7) by living out a life of total obedience to the laws of the kingdom, just as Jesus did while living on this earth.

You need to realize that God has only one law to live by, and it's applicable for all mankind, not just for Israel. Notice this principle God gives in Numbers 15:15-16:

> One ordinance shall be both for you of the congregation [covenant people], and also for the stranger [Gentile] that sojourns with you, an ordinance for ever in your generations: as you are, so shall the stranger be before the LORD.

> One law [Torah] and one manner [of living] shall be for you, and for the stranger that sojourns with you.

All the nations on earth during the millennium (thousand-year period) will learn the law (Torah) of God and be required to live by it. Notice what happens to the nations that do not obey God's commandments during the millennium:

> And it shall come to pass [during the millennium], that every one that is left of all the nations which came against Jerusalem shall even go up from year to year to worship the King, the LORD of hosts, and to keep the feast of tabernacles [see Leviticus, chapter 23, for all of God's feast days].

> And it shall be, that whoso will not come up of all the families of the earth unto Jerusalem to worship the King, the LORD of hosts, even upon them shall be no rain.

> And if the family of Egypt go not up, and come not, that have no rain; there shall be the plague, wherewith the

LORD will smite the heathen that come not up to keep the feast of tabernacles.

This shall be the punishment of Egypt, and the punishment of all nations that come not to keep the feast of tabernacles (Zech. 14:16-19).

You will need to realize that God has only one chosen people, Israel, whom He calls the "apple of his eye" (Deut. 32:10). To Israel, He says, "For you are a holy people unto the LORD your God: the LORD your God has chosen you to be a special people unto himself, above all people that are upon the face of the earth" (Deut. 7:6).

Israel is represented by the olive tree (Hosea 14:6). The olive tree is supported and nourished by the roots of Torah, which allow the tree to produce righteous fruit. Paul writes in Romans, chapter 11, about the Gentile believer (wild olive branch) being grafted into the olive tree, or Israel. He makes the argument (for those who have eyes to see) that the Gentile believer is spiritual Israel. It will be spiritual Israel who will be "the light on a hill." It will be the Bride (the firstfruits), the "jewel" of God, who comes out of spiritual Israel, who will marry Christ (Christ will only marry one of his own for He will not be "unequally yoked").

You will need to realize that it will be the Bride who will be called great in the kingdom (see Matt. 5:19), teaching the nations the Torah, the commandments of God. Are you getting the vision of the kingdom of God that you are being called into and why it is important to understand that now is the time of preparation?

Paul said in Philippians 3:14 that he pressed "toward the mark for the prize of the high calling of God in Christ Jesus." That prize is to be chosen to be the Bride of Christ, the greatest reward an individual can receive in this life.

To be called to become the Bride of Christ is a calling unlike any other. It is a calling to be holy, sanctified, set apart. That means it is a calling to be separate from organized religion or anything that might appear to be related to a false god. Yet, at the same time, it is a calling to be a "light on a hill," to let your life make a difference in other people's lives, whether it is family, friends, coworkers, and so on.

Satan has done his job well. From the very beginning of the church (the called-out ones), he has brought in deception to the point that now, in the twenty-first century, the church looks radically different from the one Christ started on the Day of Pentecost, AD 31. Jesus warned His disciples of this deception (see Matt. 24:4-5). He said to "take heed that no one deceive you." He knew that many would come, supposedly representing Him (coming in His name), but preaching a false message and "deceiving many." We see a Christian church today steeped in religious traditions that are based on pagan rituals, days, and customs. This is called confusion, "Babylon." Jesus tells His people "to come out of her [Babylon], my people, that you be not partakers of her sins" (Rev. 18:4).

Just as we learned in the previous chapter, God has established His days (not Jewish days) that He wants His people to obey. These days are declared in Leviticus, chapter 23. These days were kept by Jesus and the early church. These days have not been done away with, for they remain God's appointed times.

Your calling is to "seek first the kingdom of God and His righteousness" (Matt. 6:33); that is, to learn the ways of your Creator God, to learn of His spiritual laws that He has set in motion for your good. That is what Torah is all about. This is what the apostle John meant when he said in 1 John 2:3, "And hereby we do know that we know him [have a deep, abiding relationship with Him], if we keep his commandments." And as you learn of His ways and laws and live them, you get to know your heavenly Father more intimately and become one with Him and Jesus Christ for all eternity.

Now, back to the question at hand: "Where do I go from here?" The simple answer is to ask your heavenly Father. Go to Him in deep, earnest prayer. Trust Him to lead, guide, and direct you on the straight and narrow path that few are able to follow. Pray for wisdom. Take baby steps at first in your journey. You will be amazed at how God will link you up with divine appointments, making contact with individuals and ministries that will help you on your journey.

Know this: Satan will not make it easy for you to make these radical changes in your life. This is what Jesus meant when he said in Matthew 10:34:

> Think not that I am come to send peace on earth: I came not to send peace, but a sword.

Jesus is saying, "When you choose me and my way of living, it will bring division and discourse in the family and in other relationships" (see verses 35-39). But take heart, my friend. Your heavenly Father would not have chosen you for this journey if He knew you could not finish it. Your calling is a walk of faith. Your faith is your victory (1 John 5:4).

I can assure you beloved, that as you walk in covenant relationship with your heavenly Father, you will be richly blessed in this life beyond measure and especially in the life to come.

To help you on your journey, I recommend these resources, vital information on clean and unclean foods, on understanding God's Holy Days, on understanding what a kingdom is, on answering the question, "Should Christians be Torah observant?", and on the believer's authority:

A book by Hope Egan, entitled *Holy Cow! Does God Care about What We Eat?* (ISBN: 1-892124-19-X).

A booklet published by the Living Church of God, entitled *The Holy Days: God's Master Plan* (contact info: www.lcg.org).

A book by Myles Munroe, entitled *Rediscovering the Kingdom* (ISBN: 0-7684-2217-5).

A book by Carmen Welker, entitled *Should Christians Be Torah Observant?* (ISBN: 978-1-934916-00-1).

A booklet published by Kenneth Hagin Ministries, entitled *The Believer's Authority* (ISBN-13: 978-0-89276-406-8, ISBN-10: 0-89276-406-6).

As you can see, these resources are from different individuals and ministries, which hold to different beliefs, yet each resource is based on sound biblical truths backed up with many supporting scriptural references. (No one ministry has all truth, and my endorsement of these individuals and ministries does not mean that I agree with all their teachings and beliefs).

THE HONOR OF KINGS

The Bible tells us that "it is the glory of God to conceal a thing: but the honor of kings is to search out a matter" (Prov. 25:2). God takes pleasure in concealing nuggets of truth within His inspired written word, the Bible. The Bible is an end-time book, written specifically for those of us who are part of this end-time generation.

Truth has been hidden for millennia within the Word of God until this age, when it can be understood. For example, the prophesies in the book of Daniel were sealed "until the time of the end." Notice Daniel 12:4, 9:

> Daniel, shut up the words, and seal the book, [until] the time of the end.

> And God said, Go your way, Daniel: for the words are closed up and sealed till the time of the end.

It is now, in our end-time generation, that we understand more about end-time events than any generation before us. The same holds true for understanding the hidden truth (hidden manna) of who and what is the Bride of Christ.

This mystery is being revealed to those who have "eyes to see and ears to hear." God calls these mysteries "hidden manna" because they are hidden or concealed truths of scriptures given to the Bride. Notice Revelation 2:17, where God says to those who overcome (the Bride): "To him that overcomes will I give of the hidden manna." God is saying in no uncertain terms to the Bride: "Because of who you are, and your willingness to search out a matter, I will give you understanding of the mystery of the Bride."

Now, look at Proverbs 25:2 again. God tells us "it is the honor of Kings to search out a matter." You, who are reading this book, have been given the opportunity to search out the matter concerning the mystery of the Bride, that when understood and totally embraced will not only change your life, but will forever change your relationship with your heavenly Father. And you will be given the honor of Kings to rule and reign with Christ as His Bride.

This book is not the sum total of all there is to understanding the mystery of the Bride. It is the beginning of a lifelong journey to search out truths, not according to so-called Christian tradition, but according to the true Word of God (the Holy Bible), as the Spirit of Truth reveals it to you.

May God help you search out these nuggets as you prepare to be the Bride.

APPENDIX

GOD'S ANNUAL FEASTS

All Holy Days begin the evening before
*Passover observed previous evening

Year	First Day of Sacred Year	Passover*	Unleavened Bread	Pentecost
2018	March 17	March 30	March 31–April 6	May 20
2019	April 6	April 19	April 20–26	June9
2020	March 26	April 8	April 9–15	May 31
2021	March 14	March 27	March 28–April 3	May 16
2022	April 2	April 15	April 16–22	June 5
2023	March 23	April 5	April 6–12	May 28

Year	Feast of Trumpets	Day of Atonement	Feast of Tabernacles	Last Great Day
2018	September 10	September 19	September 24–30	October 1
2019	September 30	October 9	October 14–20	October 21
2020	September 19	September 28	October 3–9	October 10
2021	September 7	September 16	September 21–27	September 28
2022	September 26	October 5	October 10–16	October 17
2023	September 16	September 25	September 30–October 6	October 7

Printed in the United States
By Bookmasters